Daily Math
Warm-Ups
Grade Three

by
M.J. Owen

Carson-Dellosa Publishing Company, Inc.
Greensboro, North Carolina

Credits

Editors
Hank Rudisill
Amy Gamble

Cover Design
Dez Perrotti

Cover Photo
Comstock, Inc.

Layout Design
Hank Rudisill

Art Coordinator
Betsy Peninger

Artists
Jon Nawrocik
Julie Kinlaw
Mike Duggins

Printed in the USA • All rights reserved   ISBN 0-88724-819-5

Table of Contents
Daily Math Warm-Ups Grade Three

Introduction to *Daily Math Warm-Ups*

Based on standards specified by the National Council of Teachers of Mathematics (NCTM), *Daily Math Warm-Ups* will give teachers a year-long collection of challenging problems that reinforce math skills taught in the classroom. Designed around the traditional school year, the series offers 180 daily lessons (sets of five problems each) including computation, graph, and word problems. For each two-week group of lessons, an eight-problem multiple-choice assessment is provided to help you easily identify which students have mastered which concepts. The daily practice will help improve students' skills and bolster their confidence.

How to Use This Book

You can use this book in the following ways:
- Use the problems as a daily math warm-up. Make each child responsible for keeping a math journal which is checked periodically. Copy the daily lessons on transparencies. At the beginning of each class, put the problems on an overhead and give students approximately five minutes to solve the problems. When students have completed the exercise, go over the problems as a class. You can use this opportunity to discuss why some answers are correct and others are not.
- Because copying from the board or overhead is challenging for some learners, you may choose to photocopy the daily lessons for particular students, or for the entire class. Have students work on the problems at the beginning of class, then continue as described above.
- Give each student a copy of the problems near the end of class and have them turn the work in as a "Ticket Out the Door." You can then check students' work and then return their work and go over the answers at the beginning of the next class period.

Daily Math Warm-Ups includes many elements that will help students master a wide range of mathematical concepts. These include:

- 180 five-problem lessons based on standards specified by the National Council of Teachers of Mathematics

- 18 multiple-choice assessment tests in standardized-test format, to help identify concepts mastered and concepts in need of reteaching

- 12 real-world application extension activities

- A reproducible problem-solving strategy guide for students (on the inside back cover)

- Plenty of computation, graph, and word-problem solving opportunities that become more difficult as students progress through the school year

Lesson 1

1. Write the name of the ordinal number. 15th _____

2. $18 - 15 =$

3. $45 + 88 =$

4. Draw a picture, write a number sentence, and solve the problem. Sarah had 33 pieces of paper. She dropped 17 pieces of paper. How many pieces of paper does Sarah have now?

   _____

   Sarah has _____ pieces of paper now.

5. Look at the Base Ten Blocks. Write the number shown.

   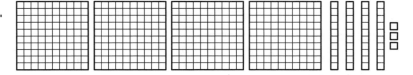

   _____

Lesson 2

1. Write the number in standard form. $1,000 + 500 + 30 + 3$ _____

2. $17 + 18 =$

3. $21 - 18 =$

4. Mary made 27 pizzas. She made 16 pepperoni pizzas. The rest were cheese pizzas. How many cheese pizzas did Mary make?

   Mary made _____ cheese pizzas.

5. Look at the picture. Write the name of the student who is sixth in line.

   _____

 Jon Dez Dion Jen Hank Sue  Joe

Lesson 3

1. Write the number in standard form. 9 hundreds, 4 tens, 7 ones

   _____

2. Write the number in standard form. 3,000 + 800 + 60 + 5 _____

3. 112 + 57 =

4. Write a number sentence and solve the problem. Martin has $0.85. He earns $1.35. How much money does Martin have now?

   _____

   Martin has _____ now.

5. Write the number seven hundred eighty-eight. _____

Lesson 4

1. Write a number sentence and solve the problem. Janisha has $2.25 in her pocket. She spends $0.75 to buy a drink. How much money does Janisha have left?

   _____

   Janisha has _____ left.

2. Write the number one thousand six hundred one.

   _____

3. 121 + 218 =

4. 88 – 33 =

5. Look at the Base Ten Blocks. Write the number shown.

   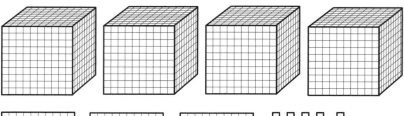

   _____

Lesson 5

1. Mary Margaret has a dog-walking business. She walked 12 dogs on Thursday, 15 dogs on Saturday, and 9 dogs on Sunday. How many dogs did Mary Margaret walk on Saturday and Sunday?

   Mary Margaret walked _____ dogs on Saturday and Sunday.

2. Write the number nine thousand six hundred fourteen.

   _____

3. $248 + 501 =$

4. $247 - 113 =$

5. In the box, draw Base Ten Blocks to show the number five hundred fifteen.

Lesson 6

1. $2,000 + 3,000 =$

2. Write the number five thousand three. _____

3. Write the number in standard form.

   $4,000 + 500 + 70 + 4$ _____

4. $137 - 84 =$

5. Draw a picture, write a number sentence, and solve the problem. Will made 9 phone calls each day for 2 days. How many phone calls did Will make in all?

   _____

   Will made _____ phone calls in all.

7

Lesson 7

1. Write the numbers in order from least to greatest. 765, 343, 123, 788, 709

_____

2. Meg did 28 push-ups on Wednesday. She did 7 fewer push-ups on Thursday. How many push-ups did Meg do on Thursday?

Meg did _____ push-ups on Thursday.

3. 191 − 68 =

4. 433 + 210 =

5. Look at the Base Ten Blocks. Write the number shown.

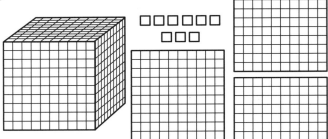

_____

Lesson 8

1. Write the numbers in order from greatest to least. 223, 675, 898, 756, 201

_____

2. The zookeeper takes 2 bags of peanuts to an elephant. There are 12 peanuts in each bag. How many peanuts does the zookeeper give to the elephant?

The zookeeper gives the elephant _____ peanuts.

3. 456 − 135 =

4. 1,001 + 2,344 =

5. Look at the Base Ten Blocks. Write the number shown.

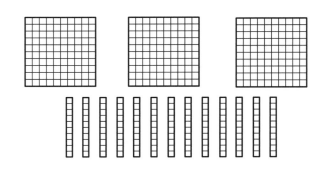

_____

Lesson 9

1. Write the number in standard form. 5,000 + 40 + 8 _____

2. Write the numbers in order from least to greatest. 801, 811, 110, 810, 708

   _____

3. Look at the number in the box. Follow the directions.
   First, circle the number in the ones place.
   Second, draw an X on the number in the tens place.
   Third, draw a line through the number in the hundreds place.
   Fourth, draw a square around the number in the thousands place.

   $$4{,}376$$

4. 417 + 303 =

5. Owen is going to visit his aunt. He travels 278 miles on Saturday. He travels 81 miles farther on Sunday than he did on Saturday. How many miles did Owen travel on Sunday?

   Owen traveled _____ miles on Sunday.

Lesson 10

1. Write the number in standard form. 7,000 + 800 + 40 + 9 _____

2. Write the name of the ordinal number. 19th _____

3. 678 – 518 =

4. 765 + 139 =

5. Write a number sentence and solve the problem. There are 221 children going on a field trip. There are 118 girls. The rest are boys. How many of the children are boys?

   _____

   There are _____ boys.

Lesson 11

1. Juana has 17 dimes, 11 quarters, and 8 pennies in her pocket. How many dimes and quarters does Juana have in her pocket?

    Juana has _____ dimes and quarters in her pocket.

2. $9 +$ _____ $= 20$

3. $15 -$ _____ $= 11$

4. $17 +$ _____ $= 22$

5. Look at the bar graph. How many more students voted for baseball and basketball than voted for football and soccer?

    _____ more students voted for baseball and basketball than for football and soccer.

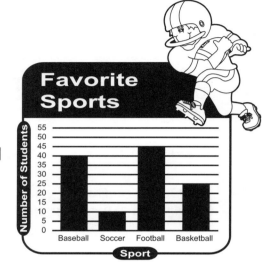

Favorite Sports

Lesson 12

1. Fill in the missing numbers to complete the pattern.

    3, 6, 9, _____, 15, _____, _____

2. Matt has 24 baseballs. He finds 15 more baseballs at the park. How many baseballs does Matt have total?

    Matt has _____ baseballs total.

3. $32 + 12 =$

4. $14 - 7 =$

5. $19 + 10 =$

Lesson 13

1. There are 15 flowers in a vase. If 9 flowers are orange and the rest are red, how many flowers are red?

   _____ flowers are red.

2. $9 + 9 =$

3. Look at the tally chart. Which color is the most popular? The least popular?

   _____ was the most popular color.

   _____ was the least popular color.

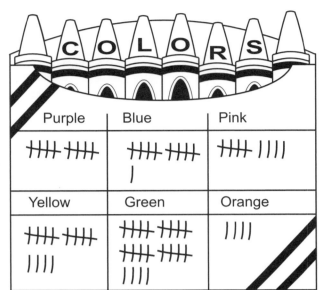

Purple	Blue	Pink
## ##	## ## #	## ####
Yellow	Green	Orange
## ## ####	## ## ## ## ####	####

4. $30 - 20 =$

5. $200 + 400 =$

Lesson 14

1. Pedro wants to play flag football with 9 of his friends. Each player needs 2 flags. How many flags are needed so that all 9 friends and Pedro can play flag football together?

   The friends need a total of _____ flags.

2. $15 + 15 =$

3. $75 + 68 =$

4. $21 - 11 =$

5. Draw the missing shapes to complete the pattern.

Lesson 15

1. There are 233 students at Marnie's school. If 112 of the students live less than 10 miles from the school and the rest of the students live more than 10 miles away from the school, how many students live more than 10 miles away from the school?

   _____ students live more than
   10 miles away from the school.

2. $5 \times 1 =$

3. $19 +$ _____ $= 23$

4. $44 + 25 =$

5. Draw a picture in the box to show the number sentence $15 - 3 =$.

Lesson 16

1. There are 128 animals at the zoo. Of those, 116 animals must be fed before 7 A.M. The rest of the animals are fed after 7 A.M. How many animals are fed after 7 A.M.?

   _____ animals are fed after 7 A.M.

2. $118 + 176 =$

3. $212 + 138 =$

4. Fill in the missing letters to complete the pattern.

   Z, Z, X, X, _____, V, T, T, _____, _____

5. $97 - 64 =$

Lesson 17

1. A total of 219 students signed up to take swimming lessons. If 174 students are under 10 years old, how many students are over 10 years old?

    _____ students are over 10 years old.

2. $72 - 12 =$

3. $44 - 28 =$

4. $314 + 266 =$

5. Draw a picture in the box to show the number sentence $9 \times 4 = .$

Lesson 18

1. If 3 students read 4 books each, how many books did the children read in all?

    The children read _____ books in all.

2. $515 + 276 =$

3. $31 - 18 =$

4. $2 \times 3 =$

5. Look at the picture. The picture shows a number sentence about how many award ribbons there are. On the line below, write the number sentence. Then, solve the problem.

    _____

    There are _____ award ribbons.

Lesson 19

1. 2 x 4 =

2. 3 x 1 =

3. 141 + 233 =

4. James is sorting laundry. He sorts 14 navy socks, 10 red socks, and 24 white socks into separate piles. How many red and white socks does James sort in all?

    James sorts a total of _____ red and white socks.

5. Fill in the missing numbers to complete the pattern.

    76, 82, 88, _____, 100, _____

Lesson 20

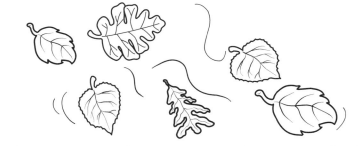

1. 0 x 4 =

2. 250 + 188 =

3. 71 – 16 =

4. Jay rakes leaves during the first week of September. He makes 3 piles of leaves. If there are 100 leaves in each pile, how many leaves are in all 3 piles total?

    There are _____ leaves in all 3 piles total.

5. Fill in the blank to complete the pattern.

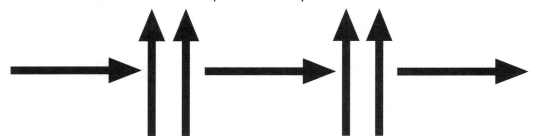

_____

Lesson 21

1. Look at the pictograph. How many children like lemon pie best?

   _____ children like lemon pie best.

2. 113 + 76 =

3. 3 x 5 =

4. Joelle has 4 flowers for herself and each of her 4 friends. How many flowers does she have in all?

   Joelle has _____ flowers.

5. Round each number to the nearest ten.

   58 _____   61 _____   85 _____

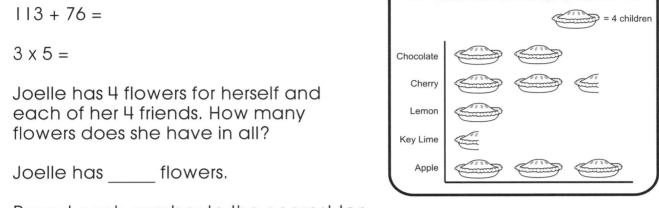

Favorite Type of Pie

= 4 children

Chocolate
Cherry
Lemon
Key Lime
Apple

Lesson 22

1. 24 – 16 =

2. 1 x 4 =

3. 212 + 116 =

4. Look at the bar graph. How many more pounds of tomatoes were sold than cucumbers?

   _____ more pounds of tomatoes were sold than cucumbers.

5. There are 315 cookies in a bowl. Macy eats 27 cookies. How many cookies are left in the bowl?

   _____ cookies are left in the bowl.

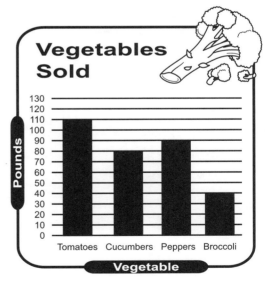

Vegetables Sold

Pounds
130
120
110
100
90
80
70
60
50
40
30
20
10
0

Tomatoes Cucumbers Peppers Broccoli

Vegetable

                   Daily Math Warm-Ups Grade 3

Lesson 23

1. Round each number to the nearest ten.
   54 _____   71 _____   86 _____

2. There are 20 people in a swimming pool. There are an equal number of swimmers in the deep end and in the shallow end of the pool. How many swimmers are in each end of the pool?

   There are _____ swimmers in each end of the pool.

3. $254 + 654 =$

4. $149 - 38 =$

5. Look at the pictograph. How many houses are there on Avenues B, C, and D?

   There are _____ houses on Avenues B, C, and D.

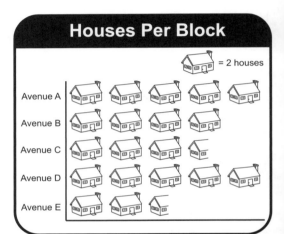

Lesson 24

1. Each of 8 friends has a button collection. Each girl has 8 buttons in her collection. How many buttons are there total in all 8 collections?

   There are _____ buttons in all 8 collections total.

2. $5 \times 3 =$

3. $37 - 14 =$

4. $22 + 303 =$

5. Look at the bar graph. How many more students are enrolled at Ridgetop than at Matadorne?

   There are _____ more students enrolled at Ridgetop than at Matadorne.

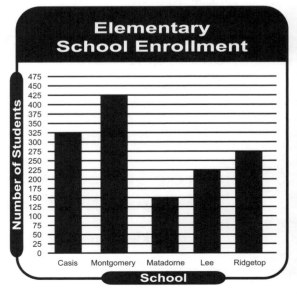

Lesson 25

1. Delena has 95 computer disks in her school box. The disks have red, blue, and green labels. If 33 of the disks have blue labels, 41 of the disks have red labels, and 21 of the disks have green labels. How many disks have red or green labels?

   _____ disks have red or green labels.

2. $9 \times 4 =$

3. $101 - 79 =$

4. $58 + 58 =$

5. Look at the pictograph. How many cans did the third graders recycle during December and February?

   The third graders recycled _____ cans during December and February.

Cans Recycled by Third Graders

November	
December	
January	
February	

○ = 10 cans

Lesson 26

1. Belinda is going to visit her sister in New York City. First, she travels 191 miles by airplane. Next, she travels 18 miles by bus and then 2 more miles by foot. How many miles does Belinda travel in all?

   Belinda travels _____ miles in all.

2. $19 + 17 =$

3. $3 \times 10 =$

4. $50 - 15 =$

5. Round each number to the nearest hundred.

   134 _____   145 _____   181 _____

Lesson 27

1. The P.E. teacher gave 6 balls to each of 6 teams. How many balls did the teacher give to the teams in all?

   The P.E. teacher gave _____ balls to the teams in all.

2. 272 + 301 =

3. 41 – 18 =

4. 6 x 3 =

5. Look at the pictograph. How many third graders' bedtimes are shown on the pictograph?

   _____ third graders' bedtimes are shown on the pictograph.

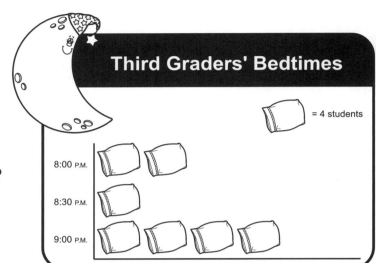

Third Graders' Bedtimes

= 4 students

8:00 P.M.

8:30 P.M.

9:00 P.M.

Lesson 28

1. It is 5 P.M. and the grocery store is very crowded. There are 9 people waiting in a checkout line. Each person is waiting to buy 4 items. How many items do the 9 people have in all?

   The 9 people have a total of _____ items.

2. 28 + 476 =

3. 334 – 211 =

4. 8 x 2 =

5. Look at the table. How many more minutes did Caroline spend running than jumping rope?

   Caroline spent _____ more minutes running than jumping rope.

| Time Caroline Spent Exercising ||
Exercise	Number of Minutes
Running	100
Jumping Rope	33
Playing Tag	65

Lesson 29

1. There are 567 people who want tickets to a concert. There are only 417 tickets available. How many people will not be able to get tickets?

   _____ people will not be able to get tickets.

2. Look at the bar graph. About how many people entered the Bake-Off in 2001 and 2002? Round each number to the nearest hundred, then add the numbers.

   About _____ people entered the Bake-Off in 2001 and 2002.

3. 5 x 5 =

4. 10 x 1 =

5. 61 – 27 =

Lesson 30

1. Look at the pictograph. How many more trees were planted on the playground in September than in November?

   _____ more trees were planted in September than November.

2. 15 + 37 + 10 =

3. 355 – 89 =

4. 281 + 335 =

5. There are 7 days in a week. There are about 4 weeks in a month. About how many days are in a month?

   There are about _____ days in a month.

19

Lesson 31

1. Melissa places 4 pictures on each of the 5 shelves in her bedroom. How many pictures does Melissa place on the shelves in all?

    Melissa places _____ pictures on the shelves in all.

2. 46 + 315 =

3. 3 x 3 =

4. 117 – 81 =

5. Look at the picture. The picture shows a number sentence about how many beads and jewels are on all of the necklaces. Write the number sentence. Then, solve the problem.

    _____

    There are _____ beads and jewels on all of the necklaces.

Lesson 32

1. Look at the table. How many pencils, notebooks, and crayons are needed?

    _____

2. 266 + 239 =

3. 401 – 29 =

4. 9 x 8 =

Grade 3 School Supply List	
Supply	Amount
Pencils	25
Markers	4
Notebooks	8
Crayons	4

5. Madeline recorded how she spent her free time one week. She spent 9 hours with friends, 6 hours doing homework, and 3 hours reading. How many more hours did Madeline spend with friends than doing homework?

    Madeline spent _____ more hours with friends.

Lesson 33

1. Mr. McKorkle gave 6 plastic necklaces to each child at his daughter's birthday party. If there were 9 children, including his daughter, at the party, how many necklaces did he hand out in all?

   Mr. McKorkle handed out _____ necklaces.

2. $19 + 21 - 6 =$

3. $6 \times 8 =$

4. $4 \times 10 =$

5. Look at the pictograph. Write a number sentence to find the number of letters mailed on Wednesday, Thursday, and Friday combined. Then, solve the problem.

   _____

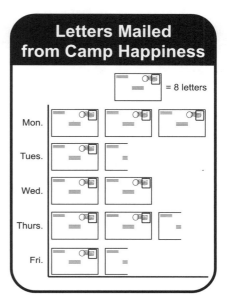

Lesson 34

1. Janet takes care of 4 horses. She is paid $8 every day. If Janet feeds each horse 2 times a day, how many times does she feed a horse during one day?

   Janet feeds a horse _____ times during one day.

2. $49 - 12 =$

3. $201 - 59 =$

4. $204 + 414 =$

5. Look at the table. How much more money did Luke spend on juice than he spent on yogurt?

   Luke spent _____ more on juice than on yogurt.

Items Luke Bought

Item	Price
Juice	$1.25
Bagel	$0.75
Newspaper	$0.50
Yogurt	$0.50

21

Name _____

Lesson 35

1. Becky has 38 ribbons for her hair. If 14 of the ribbons are striped and the rest of the ribbons are a solid color, how many of the ribbons are a solid color?

   _____ of the ribbons are a solid color.

2. 9 x 6 =

3. 49 – 8 =

4. 75 + 80 =

5. Look at the tally chart. How many wins did the Angels and Cardinals have combined?

   The Angels and Cardinals had _____ wins combined.

Team Wins	
Angels	Kangaroos
ⅢⅢ ||||| ||||
Cardinals	Score Makers
ⅢⅢ ⅢⅢ		ⅢⅢ	

Lesson 36

1. Martina is reading a book that is 267 pages long. She reads the first 99 pages on the ride home from her grandmother's house. How many pages does Martina have left to read?

   Martina has _____ pages left to read.

2. 300 + 52 =

3. 7 x 7 =

4. 444 + 279 =

5. Look at the bar graph. How many more people picked apple juice as their favorite juice than picked grape juice?

   _____ more people picked apple juice than grape juice.

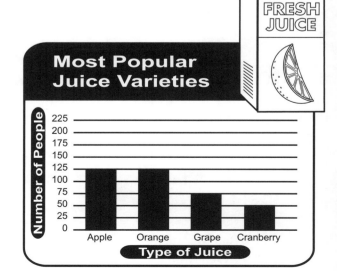

Most Popular Juice Varieties

Number of People: 225, 200, 175, 150, 125, 100, 75, 50, 25, 0

Type of Juice: Apple, Orange, Grape, Cranberry

Lesson 37

1. Look at the table. What is the total length of all four objects?

   The total length of the pencil, tack, paper clip, and eraser is _____ inches.

Length of Objects	
Object	Inches
Pencil	4
Tack	2
Paper Clip	3
Eraser	1

2. $7 \times 9 =$

3. $3 \times 4 =$

4. $11 + 4 + 18 =$

5. There are 6 groups of 5 people each working on a difficult math problem. Each group is using 2 calculators. How many calculators total are all 6 groups using?

   All six groups are using a total of _____ calculators.

Lesson 38

1. There are 19 people waiting in line for The Super Sale Store to open. Kelsey is fifth in line. How many people are behind Kelsey?

   _____ people are behind Kelsey.

2. $249 + 307 =$

3. $8 \times 8 =$

4. $133 + 76 =$

5. Look at the pictograph. How many more cars were parked on Avenue D on Thursday and Friday than on Monday and Tuesday?

   _____ more cars were parked on Avenue D on Thursday and Friday than on Monday and Tuesday.

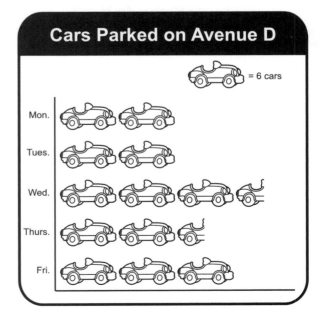

Cars Parked on Avenue D

= 6 cars

Mon.
Tues.
Wed.
Thurs.
Fri.

23

Lesson 39

1. $22 + 9 - 4 =$

2. $417 - 78 =$

3. $26 + 17 =$

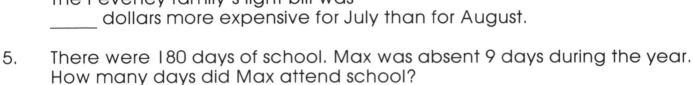

The Peveney Family's Light Bill

4. How much more expensive was the Peveney family's light bill for July than for August?

   The Peveney family's light bill was _____ dollars more expensive for July than for August.

5. There were 180 days of school. Max was absent 9 days during the year. How many days did Max attend school?

   Max attended _____ days of school.

Lesson 40

1. There are 9 rows of students performing a dance. The performance is 3 minutes long. There are 4 people in each row. How many students are performing the dance?

   _____ students are performing the dance.

2. $9 \times 7 =$

3. $2 \times 6 =$

4. $10 \times 6 =$

5. Circle the picture that shows the number sentence $5 \times 5 =$.

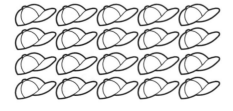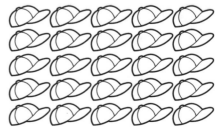

Lesson 41

1. Look at the picture of rocks in a bag. If Leslie reaches into the bag and randomly selects a rock, which type of rock is she most likely to select? Circle the letter beside the best answer.

   A. circular
   B. oval
   C. triangular
   D. rectangular

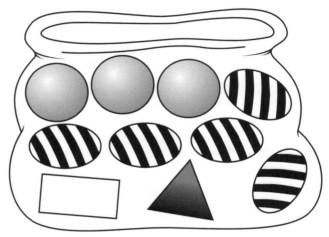

2. $37 + 222 =$

3. $211 + 418 =$

4. $149 + 121 =$

5. There were 319 people at the carnival on Saturday. On Sunday, 203 people attended the carnival. How many people attended the carnival on Saturday and Sunday combined?

   _____ people attended the carnival on Saturday and Sunday combined.

Lesson 42

1. $6 \times 5 =$

2. Fill in the missing numbers to complete the pattern.

   450, 425, 400, _____, 350, 325, 300, _____

3. Cynthia has 10 stacks of paper. There are 10 pieces of paper in each stack. How many pieces of paper does she have in all?

   Cynthia has _____ pieces of paper in all.

4. $301 - 89 =$

5. $9 \times 9 =$

Lesson 43

1. Mia is cutting a ribbon in half. The ribbon is 12 inches long, and she wants to make sure that the ribbon is divided into 2 equal parts. How many inches long should each piece of the ribbon be?

    Each piece of the ribbon should be _____ inches long.

2. 188 + 208 =

3. 7 x 6 =

4. 40 + 60 – 10 =

5. Draw the missing shapes to complete the pattern.

Lesson 44

1. Every Monday, Wednesday, and Friday, Leroy runs 4 miles. On Tuesday, he runs twice as far as on Monday. On Thursday, he runs half as far as he runs on Wednesday. Circle the letter beside the best answer.

    Today is Tuesday, so it is _____ that Leroy will run 8 miles.

    A. most likely   B. least likely   C. impossible   D. certain

2. Joey is running a marathon. A marathon is about 26 miles long. Joey takes a break for water and an energy bar after 4 miles. He then runs an additional 8 miles before taking a second break. After the second break, how many miles does Joey have left to run?

    Joey still has _____ miles left to run.

3. 3 x 4 =

4. 9 x 8 =

5. 112 – 97 =

Lesson 45

1. There are 8 bicycles available for rent at the bike shop. Each bike costs $10 per day to rent. Each bike has 2 wheels. How many wheels in all are on the bikes that are available to rent?

   There are _____ wheels on all the bikes.

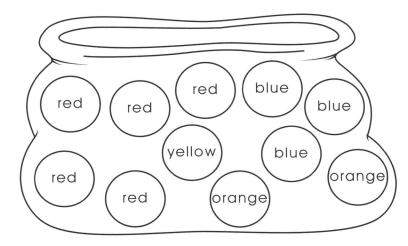

2. 19 + 107 =

3. 500 – 250 =

4. 6 x 4 =

5. Write the missing letters to complete the pattern.

   B, E, H, _____, _____, Q, T, W, _____

Lesson 46

1. There are 9 rows of computers in a busy office. There are 9 computers in each row. How many computers are in the office altogether?

   There are _____ computers in the office altogether.

2. Kayla is holding a bag of marbles. She asks Linda to randomly pick a marble from the bag. What color marble is Linda least likely to select? Circle the letter beside the best answer.

   A. orange
   B. yellow
   C. red
   D. blue

3. 26 + 4 – 9 =

4. 13 + 7 + 8 =

5. 2 + 9 + 17 =

Lesson 47

1. At the beginning of the year, there are 381 students enrolled at Mills Elementary. By the end of the year, 409 students are enrolled. How many new students enrolled during the year?

   _____ new students enrolled during the year.

2. Circle the letter beside the statement that best describes what is happening in the pattern. 47, 44, 45, 42, 43, 40, 41, 38

   A.   First, 3 is added. Then, 5 is subtracted.
   B.   First, 4 is subtracted. Then, 1 is added.
   C.   First, 3 is subtracted. Then, 1 is added.
   D.   First, 1 is subtracted. Then, 3 is added.

3. $4 \times 7 =$

4. $301 + 67 =$

5. $28 - 19 =$

Lesson 48

1. Draw the missing rectangles to complete the pattern.

  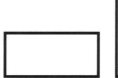 

2. $12 + 12 - 12 =$

3. $318 + 71 =$

4. $8 \times 8 =$

5. At the zoo, there are 7 habitats with 2 monkeys in each habitat. How many monkeys are in all 7 habitats?

   There are _____ monkeys in all 7 habitats.

Lesson 49

1. Look at the table. Determine the pattern and fill in the missing numbers under the heading, "Time Spent."

Time Spent Tying Shoes	
Number of Children	**Time Spent**
2	2 minutes
3	3 minutes
4	4 minutes
5	
6	6 minutes
7	

2. Maria is waiting in line to get tickets for a concert. There are 56 people in line. Maria is nineteenth in line. How many people are after Maria?

    _____ people are after Maria in line.

3. 56 + 8 =

4. 300 + 200 =

5. Estimate.
    67 + 31 is about _____ .

Lesson 50

1. Ryan's family travels 279 miles to go to the beach. Before they arrive, they stop for lunch. Ryan's mom says that they only have to travel 58 more miles before they arrive at the beach. How many miles has Ryan's family traveled so far?

    Ryan's family has traveled _____ miles so far.

2. Write the missing numbers to complete the pattern.
    87, 82, 84, 79, 81, 76, 78, _____, _____

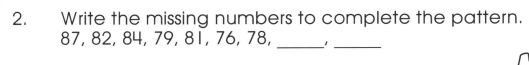

3. 44 + 15 =

4. 82 − 30 =

5. Estimate to the nearest tens place.
    75 + 79 is about _____ .

Lesson 51

1. Rashawnda is reading a book that is 584 pages long. She read 171 pages on Saturday and 207 pages on Sunday. She finished reading the book on Monday. How many pages did Rashawnda read on Monday?

   Rashawnda read _____ pages on Monday.

2. Circle the letter beside the number sentence that the picture shows.

   A. $4 \times 9 =$
   B. $4 + 9 =$
   C. $9 - 4 =$
   D. $4 \times 4 =$

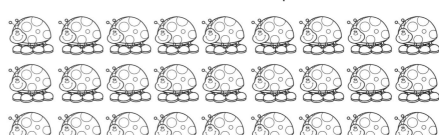

3. $213 - 157 =$

4. $211 + 337 =$

5. $3 \times 7 =$

Lesson 52

1. Fill in the blank with <, >, or = to make the number sentence true.

   289 _____ 301

2. Ben ordered 902 nails, 8 hammers, and 78 sheets of plywood to be delivered on Thursday. How many nails and sheets of plywood did Ben order in all?

   Ben ordered _____ nails and sheets of plywood in all.

3. $151 - 67 =$

4. $584 + 381 =$

5. Estimate.
   $34 + 81$ is about _____ .

Lesson 53

1. Oscar travels with a baseball team 116 days of the year. There are 365 days in a year. How many days of the year is Oscar not traveling?

   Oscar is not traveling _____ days of the year.

2. 678 + 679 =

3. 6 x 7 =

4. 8 x 2 =

5. Circle the letter beside the number sentence that the picture shows.
   A.   5 + 6 =
   B.   6 + 5 =
   C.   5 x 5 =
   D.   5 x 6 =

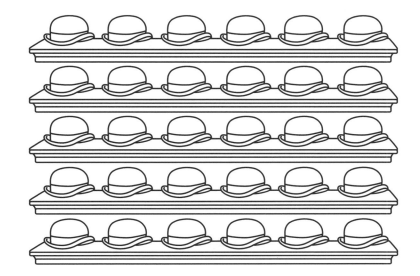

Lesson 54

1. Henry is traveling by car to visit his grandmother. He listens to 3 of his favorite CDs before he arrives at his grandmother's house. Each CD has 6 songs. How many songs does Henry listen to while he is traveling?

   Henry listens to _____ songs while he is traveling.

2. 701 + 299 =

3. 9 x 8 =

4. 10 x 5 =

5. Circle the letter beside the number sentence that the picture shows.
   A.   3 + 12 =
   B.   3 x 12 =
   C.   4 x 3 =
   D.   4 + 4 + 4 =

 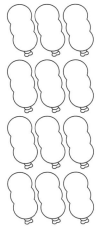 

Lesson 55

1. A family of 5 is spending 2 weeks at the beach for vacation. Each family member is taking 2 swimsuits. How many swimsuits is the family taking?

   The family is taking a total of _____ swimsuits.

2. Estimate to the nearest hundred.

   504 + 298 is about _____ .

3. Fill in the blank with <, >, or = to make the number sentence true.

   389 _____ 398

4. 3 x 8 =

5. 1,000 + 4,000 =

Lesson 56

1. Estimate to the nearest hundred.

   424 + 302 is about _____ .

2. 168 – 134 =

3. 405 + 276 =

4. 4 x 2 =

5. Annabelle mailed 10 invitations for her birthday party. She placed 4 stickers on the back of each invitation. How many stickers did Annabelle place on the invitations in all?

   Annabelle placed _____ stickers on the invitations in all.

Lesson 57

1. Naomi has 45 red beads and 69 purple beads. She loses 16 beads while making a necklace. How many beads does Naomi have now?

   Naomi has _____ beads now.

2. Write the number sentence that the picture shows. Solve.

   _____

3. 11 x 7 =

4. 3,000 + 5,000 =

5. Estimate to the nearest hundred.

   515 + 250 is about _____ .

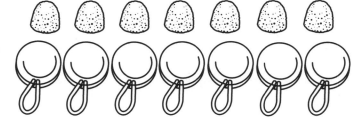
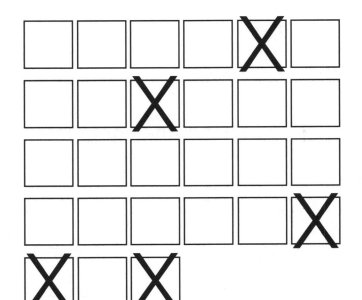

Lesson 58

1. The mail carrier delivered letters to 8 houses on a city block. He delivered 3 letters to each house. How many letters did the mail carrier deliver?

   The mail carrier delivered _____ letters.

2. 388 + 499 =

3. 5 x 0 =

4. 217 − 89 =

5. Write the number sentence that the picture shows. Solve.

   _____

33   *Daily Math Warm-Ups Grade 3*

Lesson 59

1. Write the number sentence that the picture shows. Solve.

   _____

2. 456 – 279 =

3. 1,781 + 2,000 =

4. 9 x 10 =

5. The Girls Club meets 3 times every week at their clubhouse. How many times do they meet in a 6-week period?

   The Girls Club meets _____ times during a 6-week period.

Lesson 60

1. Fill in the blank with <, >, or = to make the number sentence true.

   2,001 _____ 2,100

2. 2 x 9 =

3. 6 x 11 =

4. Draw hats in the box to show the number sentence 4 x 4 = 16.

5. Jackie has 19 dresses and 15 pairs of pants in her closet. If 9 of her dresses are blue, how many of Jackie's dresses are not blue?

   _____ of Jackie's dresses are not blue.

Lesson 61

1. If Kyle slept from 9 P.M. until 6 A.M., how many hours did he sleep in all?

    Kyle slept _____ hours total.

2. Write the number in standard form. 200 + 40 + 9

    _____

3. 4 x 3 =

4. 29 – _____ = 17

5. Draw Base Ten Blocks in the box to show 511.

Lesson 62

1. Fill in the blank with <, >, or = to make the number sentence true.

    5,015 _____ 5,011

2. Circle the even numbers.

    343   211   210   515   550   625

3. 32 – _____ = 27

4. 5,001 + 2,546 =

5. 7 x _____ = 56

Lesson 63

1. Write the numbers in order from least to greatest. 301, 310, 425, 133, 288

   _____

2. 2,675 + 3,091 =

3. Write the number in expanded form. 6,789

   _____

4. 218 − _____ = 100

5. If 10 groups of children go on a field trip, and there are 10 children in each group, how many children are there in all?

   There are _____ children in all.

Lesson 64

1. Write the number in words. 2,313

   _____

2. Latonya wrote 17 letters the first week she was at camp and 14 more letters the second week she was at camp. She ran out of stamps during the second week of camp and was unable to send 6 of the letters. How many letters did Latonya send while she was at camp?

   Latonya sent _____ letters while she was at camp.

3. 14 ÷ 7 =

4. 31 + _____ = 46

5. Look at the Base Ten Blocks. Write the number shown.

   _____

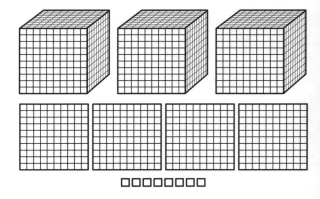

Lesson 65

1. Fill in the blank with <, >, or = to make the number sentence true.

   5,550 _____ 5,055

2. 7 x 7 =

3. 0 x 8 =

4. 21 ÷ 3 =

5. Write the numbers in order from greatest to least.

   705, 75, 806, 901, 449, 786

Lesson 66

1. 21 – _____ = 15

2. A number is between 20 and 30. It is an odd number. The sum of its digits is 5. What number is it?

   The number is _____ .

3. A total of 3,089 people voted in the city election. If 1,087 women voted in the election, and the rest of the votes were cast by men, how many men voted in the election?

   _____ men voted in the election.

4. 54 + _____ = 68

5. Write a fraction for the part that is shaded.

   _____

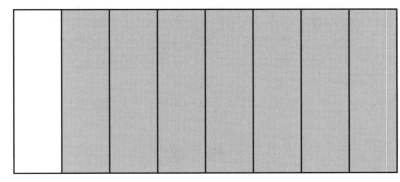

37

Lesson 67

1. $4,011 + 2,222 =$

2. $702 - 618 =$

3. Circle the even numbers.   4,054   2,011   3,787   1,298

4. Tom collects stamps. He has 36 stamps. He wants to place an equal number of stamps on each of 6 pages in his stamp collection book. How many stamps should Tom put on each page?

   Tom should put _____ stamps on each page.

5. Write the number in standard form. $7,000 + 200 + 50 + 7$

Lesson 68

1. $187 - 69 =$

2. $3,092 + 2,192 =$

3. Write the number five thousand eight hundred thirty-three.

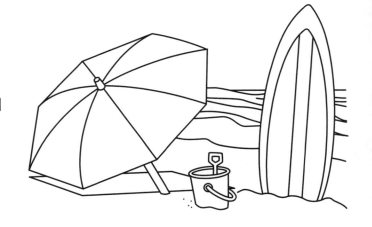

   _____

4. $8 \times 8 =$

5. In the month of April, 73 surfers decided that they would go to the beach in June. In the month of May, 13 more surfers joined the group, but 3 of the original surfers decided that they could not go in June. How many surfers were able to go to the beach in June?

   _____ surfers were able to go to the beach in June.

Lesson 69

1. A number is between 50 and 60. It is an even number. The sum of its digits equals 11. What number is it?

   The number is _____ .

2. Julie played in 9 basketball games during the month of March. She scored 8 points during each game. How many points did Julie score during March in all?

   Julie scored _____ points during March in all.

3. 7,320 + 4,567 =

4. 34 – _____ = 22

5. Circle the rectangle that shows $\frac{1}{5}$.

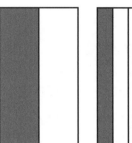
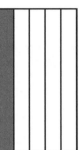
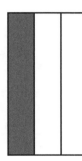

Lesson 70

1. Draw Base Ten Blocks in the box to show 420.

2. 7 x _____ = 63

3. 5 x 4 =

4. Write the numbers in order from greatest to least.

   8,765   4,323   2,132   8,011   8,310

5. Ms. Shanahan made 20 cupcakes. She divided the cupcakes equally among the students in her third-grade class. Each student received 2 cupcakes. How many students are in Ms. Shanahan's class?

   There are _____ students in Ms. Shanahan's class.

Lesson 71

1. Melanie spent 2 hours at the pool every day for 10 days. How many hours did Melanie spend at the pool over all 10 days?

   Melanie spent _____ hours at the pool over all 10 days.

2. $28 +$ _____ $= 57$

3. $3,001 + 2,998 =$

4. $256 - 179 =$

5. Look at the shape. On the first line, write the name of the shape.
   On the second line, write the number of angles that the shape has.

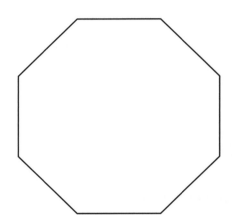

   _____

   _____

Lesson 72

1. $384 - 299 =$

2. Nancy, Jim, and Charlie spend Saturday afternoon folding laundry. There are 12 piles of laundry. Nancy, Jim, and Charlie each fold an equal number of piles of laundry. How many piles of laundry does each person fold?

   Each person folds _____ piles of laundry.

3. $6 + 8 + 17 =$

4. $6 \times 7 =$

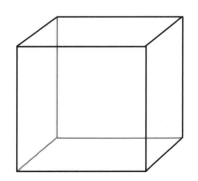

5. How many edges does the cube have?

   The cube has _____ edges.

Name _____

1. 4 x _____ = 32

2. There are 8 rows of coats hanging in the coatroom. There are 5 coats in each row. How many coats are in the coatroom?

    There are _____ coats in the coatroom.

3. Fill in the blank. A rectangular prism has _____ vertices.

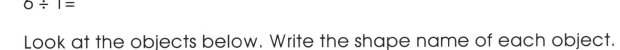

4. 6 ÷ 1 =

5. Look at the objects below. Write the shape name of each object.

_____ _____ _____

1. Circle the figure that is a polygon.

2. 8 + 9 + 7 + 1 =

3. 18 − _____ = 9

4. 21 ÷ 7 =

5. There are 1,001 people waiting in line to tour the White House. After the first 509 people get in, the tours are stopped for the day. How many people waited in line, but were unable to tour the White House?

    _____ people waited in line, but were unable to tour the White House.

Lesson 75

1. 33 + _____ = 112

2. During the year, Massey travels 3,002 miles by airplane, 1,267 miles by car, and 346 miles by bicycle. How many miles does Massey travel in all by airplane, car, and bicycle?

   Massey travels _____ miles by airplane, car, and bicycle.

3. 2 x 9 =

4. 786 – 89 =

5. How many sides does the triangle have?

   The triangle has _____ sides.

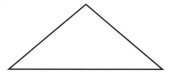

Lesson 76

1. 2,112 + 4,989 =

2. 18 ÷ 2 =

3. The school office received a box with 1,015 envelopes in it. They used 879 envelopes during the first half of the school year. How many envelopes remain in the box?

   _____ envelopes remain in the box.

4. 21 – _____ = 8

5. Circle the two figures that are congruent.

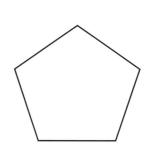
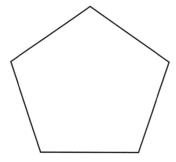

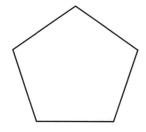

Lesson 77

1. There are 200 students enrolled in first and second grade at Catawba Elementary School. There an equal number of students enrolled in first and second grade. How many students are enrolled in the first grade?

   _____ students are enrolled in the first grade.

2. $2,099 + 4,675 =$

3. $801 - 763 =$

4. $4 \times 4 =$

5. Draw 2 points on the grid. Draw 1 point at (1,5) and 1 point at (2,4).

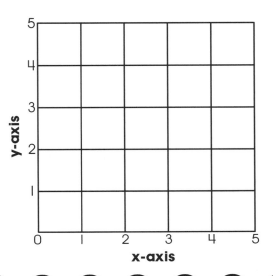

Lesson 78

1. $2,334 + 5,876 =$

2. Pierre loves cats. He has 8 cats. Each cat has 2 ears and 4 legs. How many ears do all 8 cats have?

   Pierre's cats have a total of _____ ears.

3. $51 - \underline{\quad} = 14$

4. $7 \times 8 =$

5. Circle each shape that is symmetrical.

Daily Math Warm-Ups Grade 3

Lesson 79

1. If 781 people attend a carnival on Saturday, 516 people attend on Sunday, and 622 people attend on Monday, about how many people attended the carnival on Saturday and Sunday? Estimate to the nearest hundreds place.

    About _____ people attended the carnival on Saturday and Sunday.

2. $42 \div 6 =$

3. $271 - 88 =$

4. $5,067 + 1,311 =$

5. Circle the quadrilateral that has 4 sides of the same length.

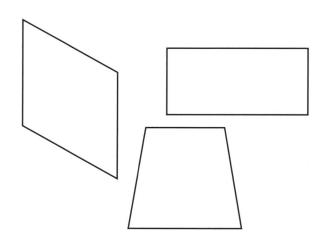

Lesson 80

1. It takes Liza 5 minutes to sharpen 8 pencils. How many pencils can Liza sharpen in 30 minutes?

    Liza can sharpen _____ pencils in 30 minutes.

2. $11 \times 8 =$

3. $4,567 + 2,344 =$

4. $1,002 - 987 =$

5. Look at how the letter was moved. Is this an example of a flip, slide, or turn?

    _____

Lesson 81

1. Circle the figure that shows correct lines of symmetry.

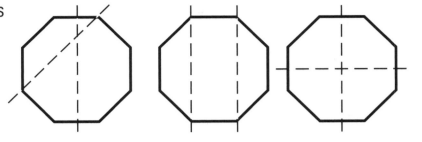

2. $9,345 + 2,091 =$

3. _____ $\times 2 = 16$

4. $40 \div 8 =$

5. Deshana and Jen spend 55 minutes planting flowers at Highland Park. Working together, they plant 1 flower every 5 minutes. How many flowers are Deshana and Jen able to plant in 55 minutes?

   Deshana and Jen are able to plant _____ flowers in 55 minutes.

Lesson 82

1. $8 \div$ _____ $= 4$

2. Teddy weighs 102 pounds. Carmen weighs 87 pounds. How much more does Teddy weigh than Carmen?

   Teddy weighs _____ pounds more than Carmen.

3. _____ $\times 7 = 56$

4. $3,021 - 456 =$

5. Circle the picture that shows a triangle with all equal sides.

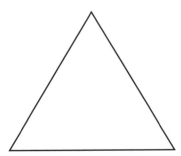
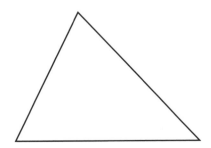
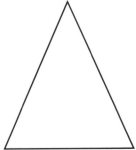

Lesson 83

1. A shape is three-dimensional, has a curved surface, and has no edges. What shape is it?

   The shape is a _____ .

2. _____ x 5 = 25

3. 2,345 + 5,467 =

4. 907 − 69 =

5. There were 2 ticket booths at the school carnival. The first ticket booth sold 4,567 tickets. The other booth sold 4,001 tickets. How many tickets did the two booths sell altogether?

   The 2 booths sold a total of _____ tickets.

Lesson 84

1. 45 ÷ 5 =

2. Nina plays 2 sets of tennis. She plays 8 games in each set. How many games did Nina play in all?

   Nina played _____ games in all.

3. 6 x 5 =

4. 907 − 314 =

5. Circle the letter that does not have a line of symmetry.

Lesson 85

1. $2,098 - 1,354 =$

2. $7,876 + 2,345 =$

3. _____ $\times 9 = 99$

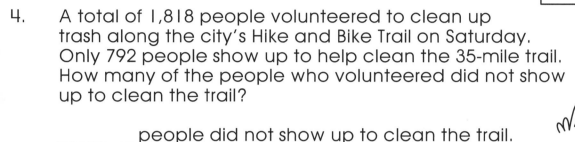

4. A total of 1,818 people volunteered to clean up trash along the city's Hike and Bike Trail on Saturday. Only 792 people show up to help clean the 35-mile trail. How many of the people who volunteered did not show up to clean the trail?

   _____ people did not show up to clean the trail.

5. A shape is three-dimensional. Each of its sides is a square, and it has 8 vertices. What shape is it?

   The shape is a _____ .

Lesson 86

1. $7 \times$ _____ $= 14$

2. $2,013 - 899 =$

3. $5,786 + 6,897 =$

4. Leanne orders 50 balloons for the school dance. She wants to put the balloons in groups of 5 around the school cafeteria. How many groups of balloons is Leanne able to make?

   Leanne is able to make _____ groups of balloons.

5. Look at the picture. List the 3 shapes that were used to draw the birdhouse.

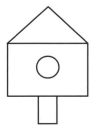

_____   _____   _____

Lesson 87

1. There are 12 ducks getting ready to dive into the pond. Each duck has 7 ducklings. The ducklings are also ready to dive into the pond. How many ducks and ducklings are ready to dive into the pond in all?

    _____ ducks and ducklings are ready to dive into the pond.

2. $167 + \_\_\_\_ = 201$

3. $\_\_\_\_ \times 15 = 30$

4. $2{,}314 - 578 =$

5. Write the name of a shape you could make by putting these triangles together.

    _____

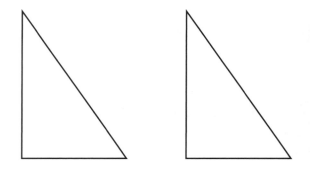

Lesson 88

1. $6 \times \_\_\_\_ = 72$

2. $15 \div 3 =$

3. $3{,}026 - 389 =$

4. A large company received 1,001 phone calls on Tuesday and 979 phone calls on Wednesday. How many more phone calls did the company receive on Tuesday than on Wednesday?

    The company received _____ more phone calls on Tuesday.

5. In the second box, draw a figure that is congruent to the triangle in the first box.

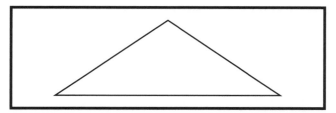 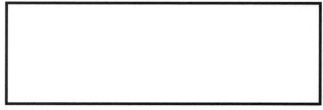

Lesson 89

1. Brooke fished for 3 hours each day for 11 days. She caught a total of 7 fish each day she went fishing. How many fish did Brooke catch during all 11 days?

    Brooke caught _____ fish during all 11 days.

2. 5,786 + 2,987 =

3. 2,345 – 2,146 =

4. 279 – _____ = 35

5. In the second box, draw a figure that is congruent to the hexagon in the first box.

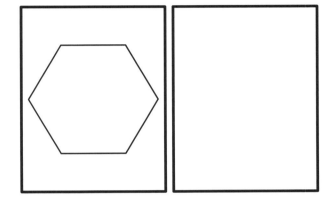

Lesson 90

1. Rami buys 12 cases of water for field day. There are 8 bottles of water in each case. How many bottles of water are there in all 12 cases?

    There are _____ bottles of water in all 12 cases.

2. 4,016 – 2,345 =

3. 10 x _____ = 90

4. 772 – _____ = 449

5. Look at the 2 rectangles below. Write whether they are congruent, similar, both, or neither on the line under the boxes.

Lesson 91

1.   The Lions baseball team plays 3 baseball games every weekend. There are 4 weekends during the month of June. How many baseball games do the Lions play during the month of June?

The Lions play _____ baseball games during the month of June.

2. $4 \times 7 =$

3. $3,456 - 1,678 =$

4. $9 \times \underline{\quad} = 99$

5.   Draw an object in the box that has at least 1 line of symmetry.

Lesson 92

1.   On Monday, Antonio checks out 12 books at the library. Each book that he checks out has 75 pages. On Wednesday, Antonio returns 5 books and checks out an additional 9 books. On Friday, he returns 3 books and checks out 1 additional book. How many books does Antonio have checked out on Friday?

Antonio has _____ books checked out on Friday.

2. $45 \div \underline{\quad} = 9$

3. $8,765 + 4,567 =$

4. $439 - \underline{\quad} = 211$

5.   Write the name of the shape on the line.

_____

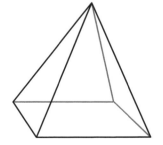

Lesson 93

1. Bonnie and Randall record the number of miles they travel each year by plane. The first summer that they recorded this information, they traveled 1,987 miles. The second summer, they traveled a distance of 2,002 miles, and the third summer, they traveled a distance of 1,345 miles. How many miles did Bonnie and Randall travel during all 3 summers?

   Bonnie and Randall traveled a distance of _____ miles.

2. $76 +$ _____ $= 178$

3. $8 \times 3 =$

4. $18 \div 3 =$

5. Look at the picture. Circle the word that correctly describes the relationship between Book A and Book B.
   turn   flip   slide

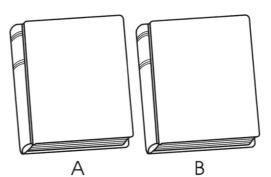

A   B

Lesson 94

1. A group of 10 third graders are making penguins using film canisters. Each third grader needs 1 film canister, 2 wiggle eyes, and 1 piece of construction paper. How many items do all 10 third graders need for the penguin project?

   The 10 third graders need a total of _____ items for the penguin project.

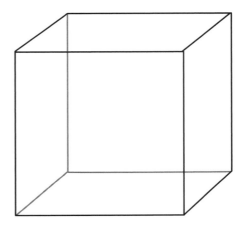

2. $3,456 - 2,768 =$

3. $134 + 271 - 26 =$

4. $12 \times 4 =$

5. Look at the cube.

   The cube has _____ faces and _____ edges.

Lesson 95

1. Emma has 50 pictures in a box. She wants to put an equal number of pictures on each of the 10 pages of her photo album. How many pictures should Emma put on each page?

   Emma should put a total of _____ pictures on each page.

2. $154 - \_\_\_\_ = 53$

3. $4 \times 8 =$

4. $22 \div 2 =$

5. Circle the number that has a line of symmetry.

Lesson 96

1. A group of 6 families attended a basketball game together. After the game, they went out to dinner. If there are 7 people in each family, how many people went to dinner?

   _____ people went to dinner.

2. $116 + 112 =$

3. $7 \times 9 =$

4. $24 \div 6 =$

5. Write the name of the shape on the line.

   _____

Lesson 97

1. Tayshaun has 2 pairs of pants hanging in his closet. Each pair of pants has 2 pockets. How many pockets are there in all?

   There are _____ pockets in all.

2. $2{,}005 - 1{,}345 =$

3. $4{,}567 + 2{,}324 =$

4. $12 \times \underline{\quad} = 48$

5. Circle the 2 shapes that are congruent.

  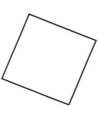

Lesson 98

1. Carrie loves to go on long bike rides. She bikes 72 miles the first weekend and 118 miles the second weekend. How many miles farther did Carrie ride on the second weekend?

   Carrie rode _____ miles farther on the second weekend.

2. $6 \times 9 =$

3. $36 \div 6 =$

4. $780 - 644 =$

5. A shape has 4 equal sides and is a polygon. Draw the shape in the box. Write the name of the shape below.

   _____

Lesson 99

1. A total of 876 students enrolled at Mount Bonnell Middle School. By the end of the semester, an additional 56 students had enrolled and 81 other students had left Mount Bonnell to attend another middle school. How many students were enrolled at the end of the semester?

    _____ students were enrolled at the end of the semester.

2. $8 \div 2 =$

3. $8 \times$ _____ $= 40$

4. $64 + 18 =$

5. Look at the sphere.
    How many vertices does a
    sphere have? _____

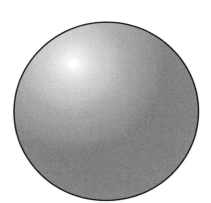

Lesson 100

1. Vanessa has 59 scarves in her closet. In all, 14 of the scarves are red, 29 of the scarves are striped, and the remaining scarves are white. How many of Vanessa's scarves are white?

    _____ of Vanessa's scarves are white.

2. $1,786 - 456 =$

3. $3 \times 3 =$

4. $100 \div 10 =$

5. Circle the figure that does not have a base.

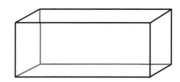  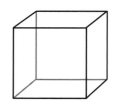 

Lesson 101

1. Jonathan weighs 182 pounds. Paige weighs 97 pounds, and Anna weighs 64 pounds. How much more does Jonathan weigh than both Paige and Anna combined?

   Jonathan weighs _____ more than Paige and Anna combined.

2. $415 + 78 - 32 =$

3. $9 \div 3 =$

4. $1,801 - 709 =$

5. What is the perimeter of the octagon?

   _____ inches

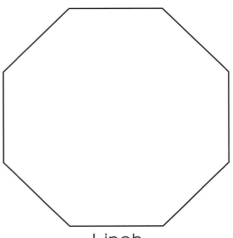

1 inch

Lesson 102

1. Circle the best answer. A baseball bat is about $2\frac{1}{2}$ _____ long.

   inches   yards   feet   miles

2. Jordan is studying for the school spelling bee. She is memorizing a list of words. The list of words is set up in 8 columns. There are 8 words in each column. How many words in all does Jordan need to study?

   Jordan needs to study _____ words.

3. $56 \div 8 =$

4. $18 \div 2 =$

5. $2,345 - 867 =$

Lesson 103

1. Hunter collects bottle caps. He has 761 bottle caps in his collection. He keeps his collection in 5 boxes. He loses 38 bottle caps when he is moving. His best friend gives him 17 bottle caps that he collected on a trip. How many bottle caps does Hunter have now?

   Hunter has _____ bottle caps now.

2. Toni is going on a trip at 3:15. She needs to allow 1 hour to pack, 30 minutes to eat, and 1 hour to straighten her room. What time does Toni need to start preparing so that she will be ready to leave at 3:15? Draw the time on the clock and write the time on the line. _____

3. $5,004 + 1,273 =$

4. $212 - 87 =$

5. $21 \div 7 =$

Lesson 104

1. Kellie is going to the beach. First, she walks 3 miles to the train station. She travels 31 miles by train. Then, she walks an additional 4 miles. Later, she takes a boat 17 miles to get to where she is staying. How many more miles did Kellie travel by boat and train than she walked?

   Kellie traveled _____ more miles by boat and train than she walked.

2. $74 - 19 =$

3. $213 - 87 =$

4. $10 \times 1 =$

5. What is the area of the square?

   _____ square inches

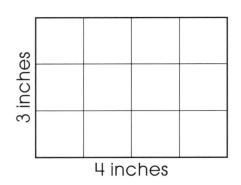

3 inches

4 inches

Lesson 105

1. Mountain View Elementary orders 1,401 calculators for students in grades 1 through 5. When the calculators arrive, it is determined that 109 of the calculators do not work. How many calculators work?

    _____ calculators work.

2. $4 \times 0 =$

3. $501 - 36 =$

4. $100 \div 20 =$

5. Look at the picture. How many inches long is the tape?

    The tape is _____ inches in length.

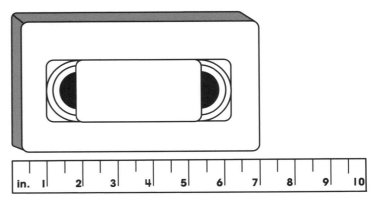

Lesson 106

1. Josie has 45 pieces of candy. She wants to put the candy in 9 bags. She plans to put an equal amount of candy in each bag. How many pieces of candy does Josie need to put in each bag?

    Josie needs to put _____ pieces of candy in each bag.

2. $4,001 - 2,998 =$

3. $12 \times 3 =$

4. $60 \div 5 =$

5. What is the volume of the cube?

    _____ cubic units

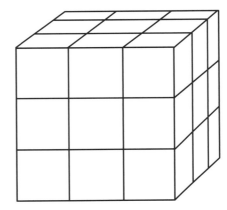

Lesson 107

1. John runs 3 miles 3 times every week. How many miles does John run in 6 weeks?

    John runs _____ miles in 6 weeks.

2. Look at the picture. About how much water will the bucket hold?
    Circle the best answer.

    5 inches   5 pounds

    5 ounces   5 gallons

3. $3,004 + 3,114 =$

4. $786 - 59 =$

5. $3 \times 4 =$

Lesson 108

1. How many ounces are in 2 pounds?

    There are _____ ounces in 2 pounds.

2. $5 \times 5 =$

3. $6 \div 3 =$

4. $401 - 287 =$

5. Chelsea uses 2 cups of chocolate chips for each batch of cookies. It takes her about 1 hour to make each batch of cookies. She makes a total of 4 batches of cookies for the school bake sale. How many cups of chocolate chip cookies does Chelsea use in all?

    Chelsea uses _____ cups of chocolate chips in all.

Lesson 109

1. On Friday, 3,005 people went to Fun Land Amusement Park. On Saturday, 2,345 people went to the park. How many people in all went to Fun Land Amusement Park over the two days?

   _____ people in all went to Fun Land Amusement Park.

2. $6 \times 6 =$

3. $4,007 + 1,111 =$

4. $782 - \underline{\quad\quad} = 567$

5. Circle the picture that shows an equilateral triangle.

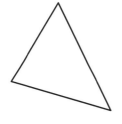 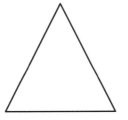 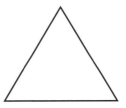

Lesson 110

1. Zach has 3 shelves of spices in his pantry. He has 16 spices on each shelf. How many spices are in Zach's pantry?

   Zach has a total of _____ spices in his pantry.

2. Write the name of the shape on the line.

   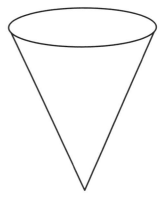

3. $63 \div 7 =$

4. $9 \times 9 =$

5. $4,878 + 2,009 =$

Lesson 111

1. $25 \div 5 =$

2. Billy is able to write 11 words a minute. How many words is he able to write in 9 minutes?

    Billy is able to write _____ words in nine minutes.

3. $387 + 2,004 =$

4. $302 - 178 =$

5. Look at the clock. Betsy arrived at the bus stop 45 minutes ago. What time did Betsy arrive at the bus stop?

    _____

Lesson 112

1. Virginia wants to make cookies for all the students in the third grade. There are 81 students in the third grade. If there are 9 cookies in each batch, how many batches will Virginia need to make so that all of the third graders get at least 1 cookie?

    Virginia will need to make at least _____ batches of cookies.

2. $6 \times 4 =$

3. $16 \div 4 =$

4. $179 + 564 - 81 =$

5. Look at the picture. About how much liquid will the glass hold? Circle the best estimate.

    1 cup   1 meter   1 gallon

Lesson 113

1. The basketball team won 114 games during the regular season. They lost 43 games. How many more games did the basketball team win than they lost?

   The basketball won _____ more games than they lost.

2. 12 x 6 =

3. 701 + 495 − 17 =

4. 14 ÷ 7 =

5. Look at the temperature on the thermometer. Circle the pictures that show the clothes Tim might wear to be comfortable at this temperature.

Lesson 114

1. Libby, Beth, Mike, Ginger, and Paul are dividing 30 cards. They want to make sure that each person in their group gets an equal number of cards. How many cards should each person get?

   Each person should get _____ cards.

2. 7,006 − 2,000 =

3. 6 x _____ = 60

4. 5,786 + 3,456 =

5. What is the area of the rectangle?

   _____ square units

8 units

4 units

Lesson 115

1. A food stand sold 457 hamburgers, 299 hot dogs, and 308 slices of pizza on a busy Saturday afternoon. How many more hamburgers than slices of pizza did the stand sell?

   The food stand sold _____ more hamburgers than slices of pizza.

2. $33 + 406 - 208 =$

3. $1,675 - 908 =$

4. $5 \times 11 =$

5. What is the volume of the shape?

   _____ cubic units

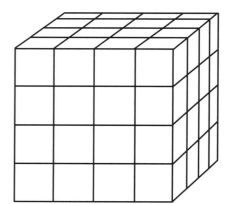

Lesson 116

1. A toy store was open from 9 A.M. to 5 P.M. every day of the week. On Thursday, the phone rang a total of 40 times during the entire day. If the phone rang an equal number of times each hour, how many times did the phone ring each hour?

   The toy store's phone rang _____ times every hour.

2. $27 \div 9 =$

3. $4,354 + 2,123 =$

4. $345 + 654 + 987 =$

5. What is the perimeter of the shape?

   _____ centimeters

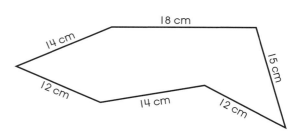

Lesson 117

1. There are 12 sets of swings at the park. Each set of swings has 5 swings. How many swings are on all 12 sets total?

    There are _____ swings on all 12 sets total.

2. 9,878 + 987 + 765 =

3. 2,221 − 498 =

4. 12 ÷ 6 =

5. How many inches long is the nail?

    The nail is _____ inches long.

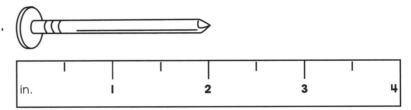

Lesson 118

1. A total of 589 kids played in the Happy Hills Soccer League. If 125 of the players have never played soccer before, how many of the players have played soccer before?

    _____ of the players have played soccer before.

2. 89 + 1,609 + 546 =

3. 12 x 2 =

4. 42 ÷ 6 =

5. About how much does a baseball weigh? Circle the best answer.

    5 liters   5 tons   5 kilograms   5 inches

Lesson 119

1. An airline pilot traveled 2,003 miles on Wednesday, 1,343 miles on Thursday, and 1,009 miles on Friday. How many miles did the airline pilot travel in all?

   The airline pilot traveled a total of _____ miles.

2. $4,657 - 809 =$

3. $344 + 566 + 806 =$

4. $20 \times 4 =$

5. 8 pints = _____ quarts

Lesson 120

1. Hannah spends 2 hours at ballet class every day. She attends ballet class every day in November. There are 30 days in the month of November. How many hours does Hannah spend in ballet class during the month of November?

   Hannah spends _____ hours in ballet class during the month of November.

2. $80 \div 10 =$

3. $9 \times 8 =$

4. $25 \times 4 =$
   (Hint: There are 4 quarters in 1 dollar.)

5. Look at the clock. What time will it be in 2 hours and 25 minutes?

   _____

Lesson 121

1. The High Fliers Acrobat Team performed on Thursday, Friday, and Saturday nights. On Thursday night, 1,709 people attended the show. On Friday, 2,456 people attended the show. On Saturday, 3,456 people attended the show. How many more people attended the show on Saturday night than on Thursday night?

   _____ more people attended the show on Saturday night than on Thursday night.

2. 3,234 + 12,876 =

3. 711 – 496 =

4. 16 ÷ 2 =

5. Look at the picture. On the line, write the fraction that represents this decimal (.20).

   _____

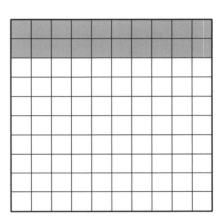

Lesson 122

1. There are 4 friends playing a game with marbles. If the players divide 48 marbles equally, how many marbles should each player get?

   Each player should get _____ marbles.

2. 7,004 + 3,256 =

3. 153 + 117 – 27 =

4. 35 ÷ 1 =

5. Look at the Base Ten Blocks. Write the number shown.

   _____

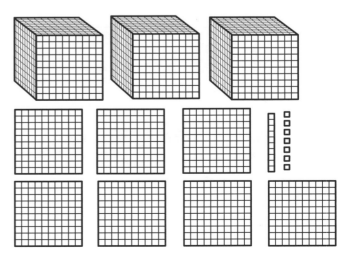

65

Lesson 123

1. $55 + 119 - 71 =$

2. $2,878 - 1,907 =$

3. Marty has $48.17. She spends $18.50 on a new album for her sticker collection. She then earns $7.25 for helping her mom clean house. How much money does Marty have now?

   Marty has _____ now.

4. Write the number one hundred thousand, six hundred forty-five.

5. Put the numbers in order from greatest to least. 701, 876, 544, 801, 717

Lesson 124

1. The school cafeteria uses 9 dozen eggs every week. There are 12 eggs in a dozen. How many eggs does the school cafeteria use every week?

   The school cafeteria uses _____ eggs every week.

2. Put the numbers in order from least to greatest. 333, 208, 359, 201, 117

3. $2 \times 5 =$

4. $8,002 + 2,988 =$

5. Look at the Base Ten Blocks. Write the number shown.

   _____

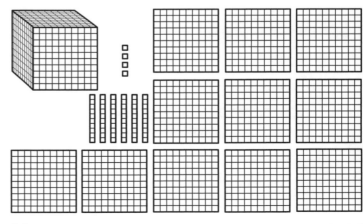

Lesson 125

1. Ricardo is trying to memorize his multiplication facts. He memorizes 5 facts every day for 12 days. How many facts can Ricardo memorize in 12 days?

   Ricardo can memorize _____ facts in 12 days.

2. Circle the even numbers.   345   567   202   313   404

3. $4 \div 1 =$

4. $620 - 515 =$

5. Shade $\frac{7}{8}$ of the rectangle.

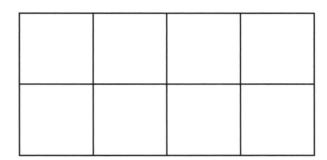

Lesson 126

1. Put the numbers in order from greatest to least.
   880, 818, 808, 709, 811, 756

   _____

2. The second graders at Forest Trails Elementary School recycled 3,567 cans during May and 3,019 cans during June. How many more cans did the second graders recycle during May?

   The second graders recycled _____ more cans during May.

3. $8 \times 8 =$

4. $4,012 + 17,006 =$

5. Draw Base Ten Blocks in the box to show 903.

Lesson 127

1. Lynn has $78.18 at the beginning of June. During June, she spends $5.75 on a new book and $21.50 visiting an amusement park. How much money does Lynn have at the end of June?

    Lynn has _____ at the end of June.

2. Circle the odd numbers.

    677   413   200   970   644

3. 708 − 559 =

4. 4 × 11 =

5. 36 ÷ 4 =

Lesson 128

1. Circle the fraction that is equivalent to $\frac{1}{2}$.

    $\frac{1}{3}$ $\frac{2}{4}$ $\frac{7}{8}$

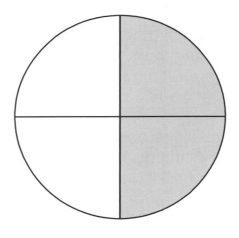

2. 5 × 4 =

3. 4,014 − 3,961 =

4. 2,879 + 5,658 =

5. Write the number fifteen thousand, three hundred two.

    _____

Lesson 129

1. Henry found 79 shells on the beach. He gave his mom 34 shells. Later, Henry found 81 more shells. How many shells does Henry have now?

   Henry has _____ shells now.

2. Put the numbers in order from greatest to least. 515, 505, 123, 414, 568

   _____

3. $18 \div 3 =$

4. $9,454 - 6,009 =$

5. Look at the Base Ten Blocks. Subtract 287 from the total value. Then, on the line below the Base Ten Blocks, write and solve the problem.

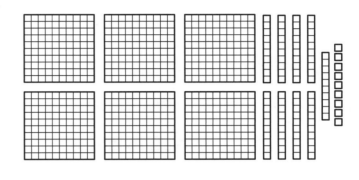

Lesson 130

1. Malik mows lawns during spring break. On Monday, he earns $18.25. On Tuesday he earns $21.75 and on Friday he earns $15.00. How much money does Malik earn in all?

   Malik earns _____ in all.

2. $2,001 + 3,456 =$

3. $12 \times 11 =$

4. Write the number two hundred thousand, six hundred eighty-five.

   _____

5. In each of the following numbers, draw an X over the digit in the hundreds place.

   701   3,456   1,098

Lesson 131

1. Claremont Elementary has 4 third-grade classes. There are 12 students in each class. How many third-grade students are in all 4 classes?

    There are _____ students in all 4 classes.

2. $18 + 9 - 6 =$

3. $9 \times 9 =$

4. $6,657 + 2,098 =$

5. Look at the pictograph. Which month had twice as many sunny days as July?

    _____ had twice as many sunny days as July.

Lesson 132

1. Dan has 100 colored beads. He wants to divide the beads equally between himself and 9 friends. How many beads will each person get?

    Each person will get _____ beads.

2. $33 + 47 - 9 =$

3. $7 \times 6 =$

4. $32 \div 4 =$

5. Look at the bar graph. How many more children attended the Fall Festival on Saturday than on Friday?

    _____ more children attended the Fall Festival on Saturday than on Friday.

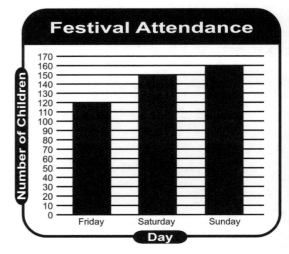

Lesson 133

1. Paul has 6 shirts in his closet. He bought 3 ties to go with each shirt. How many ties did Paul buy in all?

   Paul bought _____ ties in all.

2. 401 + 398 + 78 =

3. 675 + 223 + 117 =

4. 6 x 9 =

5. Look at the table. Based on the information in the table, which day was the warmest?

   _____ was the warmest.

Weather in My City	
Day of the Week	**Temperature**
Monday	67° F
Tuesday	65° F
Wednesday	74° F
Thursday	81° F
Friday	68° F

Lesson 134

1. Nikki collects magazines about arts and crafts. She has a total of 389 magazines. She has 87 magazines that are not about arts and crafts, so she recycles them. How many magazines does Nikki have now?

   Nikki has _____ magazines now.

2. 8 x _____ = 24

3. 12 x 8 =

4. 50 ÷ 5 =

5. Look at the tally chart. How many times total did Beka go running during September, October, and November?

   Beka went running _____ times during September, October, and November.

Number of Times Beka Ran	
September	
卌 卌 卌 卌 l	
October	November
卌 卌 卌 l	卌 卌 卌 卌 卌 ll

Lesson 135

1. A store has 297 red hats and 303 blue hats for sale. How many red hats and blue hats total does the store have for sale?

   The store has _____ total red hats and blue hats for sale.

2. $10 \div 10 =$

3. $6{,}876 - 4{,}345 =$

4. $11 \times 11 =$

5. Look at the pictograph. How many more votes did Nancy and Hector get than Fred and Ramon?

   Nancy and Hector got _____ more votes than Fred and Ramon.

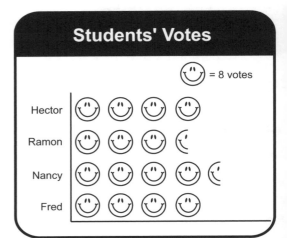

Lesson 136

1. $7{,}876 + 5{,}676 =$

2. Candice slept 8 hours for 5 days in a row. How many hours did Candice sleep over all 5 days?

   Candice slept _____ hours over all 5 days.

3. $5{,}409 - 4{,}987 =$

4. $8 \times 2 =$

5. Look at the table. Based on the information in the table, circle the letter beside the statement that is true.

Number of Boys and Girls in Art Class		
Grade	Boys	Girls
Grade 3	18	18
Grade 4	12	15
Grade 5	14	10

   A. There are fewer girls than boys in Art class.
   B. There are more students in Music class.
   C. There is an even number of girls and boys in Grade 4.
   D. There is an even number of girls and boys in Grade 5.

Lesson 137

1. At the Farmer's Market, Jane sold 12 pounds of peaches every hour. How many pounds of peaches did Jane sell during a 6-hour workday?

    Jane sold _____ pounds of peaches.

2. $7,898 - 6,789 =$

3. $410 + 314 - 88 =$

4. $9 \times 8 =$

5. Look at the bar graph. How many more trains passed through the station at 7 A.M. and 6 P.M. than at 12 noon?

    _____ more trains passed through the station at 7 A.M. and 6 P.M than at 12 noon.

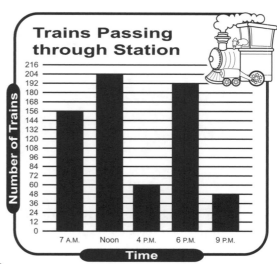

Lesson 138

1. The teachers at Canyon Lakes Elementary School bought 1,016 bottles of water for field day. The students drank 987 bottles of water. How many bottles of water are left?

    _____ bottles of water are left.

2. $10 \times 10 =$

3. $12 \times 12 =$

4. $903 + 217 - 68 =$

5. Look at the tally chart. Ms. Dunn and Mr. Owen recorded the number of soccer games each of their classes won against each other. How many total games did the classes play?

    The classes played a total of _____ soccer games against each other.

Number of Wins	
Ms. Dunn	Mr. Owen
卌 卌 卌 卌 卌 |||	卌 卌 卌 卌 卌 卌 卌 卌 卌 ||

Lesson 139

1. Look at the pictograph. How many more miles did Team 3 canoe than Teams 1 and 2 combined?

    Team 3 canoed _____ more miles than Teams 1 and 2 combined.

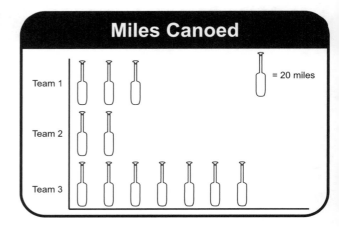

Miles Canoed

Team 1

Team 2

Team 3

= 20 miles

2. 15,989 + 4,567 =

3. 7,098 − 4,304 =

4. 85 + 4,567 =

5. There are 24 students in a gym class. If the children are standing in pairs, how many pairs of students are there?

    There are _____ pairs of students in the gym class.

Lesson 140

1. The school auditorium has 12 rows of chairs. Each row has 10 chairs. How many chairs are in all 12 rows?

    There are _____ chairs in all 12 rows.

2. 16,789 + 12,897 =

3. 9 x 11 =

4. 50 ÷ 5 =

5. Look at the bar graph. How many more students ride the bus than walk or bike to school?

    _____ more students ride the bus than walk or bike to school.

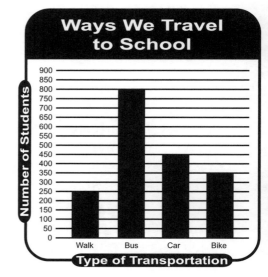

Ways We Travel to School

Lesson 141

1. 403 − 27 =

2. 2,876 + 34,657 =

3. Fill in the missing numbers to complete the pattern.

    470, 440, 410, _____, 350, _____

4. 20 x 4 =

5. Cindy spent 5 quarters every time she visited the candy store. She made 9 visits during the month of March. How many quarters did Cindy spend at the candy store during March?

    Cindy spent _____ quarters at the candy store during March.

Lesson 142

1. A total of 2,406 students bought tickets to the Rock and Roll Picnic. If 1,082 of them were boys and the rest were girls, how many girls bought tickets to the Rock and Roll Picnic?

    _____ girls bought tickets to the Rock and Roll Picnic.

2. 807 − 59 =

3. Estimate to the nearest hundred.

    501 + 457 is about _____ .

4. 32 + 15 − 11 =

5. Fill in the missing letter to complete the pattern.

    A, Z, C, Z, E, Z, _____, Z, I, Z, K, Z

Lesson 143

1. A total of 388 students entered a poster contest. If 5 children are given prizes, how many children are not given prizes?

   _____ children are not given prizes.

2. $4 \times 5 =$

3. Estimate to the nearest ten.

   $53 + 61$ is about _____ .

4. $18 \div 3 =$

5. Circle all of the odd numbers in the box.

   202   213
   654   788
   908   875

Lesson 144

1. $30 \times 3 =$

2. $9 \times 9 =$

3. Draw the missing shapes to complete the pattern.

4. $765 + 6,546 =$

5. Ben has 22 multiplication flash cards. He divides the flash cards equally with his brother. How many flash cards does each boy have?

   Ben and his brother each have _____ flash cards.

Lesson 145

1. Estimate to the nearest hundred.

   781 + 654 is about _____ .

2. Allison has saved $38.75. She decides to buy a doll that costs $15.49. Later, she earns an additional $11.00 for watering her neighbor's plants. How much money does Allison have now?

   Allison has _____ now.

3. 8,876 − 4,345 =

4. 40 ÷ 10 =

5. Write the missing numbers to complete the pattern.

   64, 62, 60, 58, _____, 54, 52, _____, _____

Lesson 146

1. Estimate to the nearest ten.

   701 + 638 is about _____ .

2. 13 x 2 =

3. 24 ÷ 8 =

4. Oliver plays 16 games of tennis. He wins half of the games he plays. How many games does Oliver win?

   Oliver wins _____ tennis games.

5. Jeremy is counting a certain kind of coin. He counts these amounts: $0.75, $1.00, $1.25, $1.50. Circle the kind of coin that Jeremy is counting.

   penny   nickel   dime   quarter

Lesson 147

1. $789 - 49 =$

2. Estimate to the nearest hundred.

   $876 - 465$ is about _____ .

3. $7 \times 6 =$

4. Fill in the missing numbers to complete the pattern.

   525, 475, 425, _____, 325, _____, _____

5. A group of 18 students perform in a piano recital. Half of the students perform before the intermission and half perform after the intermission. How many students perform before the intermission?

   _____ students perform before the intermission.

Lesson 148

1. A total of 9 airplanes are on the runway. Each airplane has 4 wheels and 2 wings. How many wheels are on all 9 airplanes?

   There are _____ wheels on all 9 airplanes.

2. $989 - 345 =$

3. $3,456 - 2,009 =$

4. $7,456 + 4,567 =$

5. Fill in the blanks to complete the pattern.

Lesson 149

1. Estimate to the nearest hundred.

   2,345 + 678 is about _____ .

2. 15 x 2 =

3. 36 ÷ 6 =

4. Fill in the missing letters to complete the pattern.

   A, A, B, _____, _____, D, E, E, _____, G, G, H

5. At the city's yearly pancake breakfast, 8 chefs made a total of 3,011 pancakes. If only 2,987 of the pancakes are eaten, how many pancakes are left over?

   _____ pancakes are left over.

Lesson 150

1. A group of 27 people are waiting in the lunch line. Jack is ninth in line. How many people are behind Jack?

   _____ people are behind Jack.

2. 40 x 5 =

3. 786 + 456 – 64 =

4. 1,000 x 1 =

5. Draw the missing shapes to complete the pattern.

Lesson 151

1. There are 17 children in Mr. Spencer's third-grade class. Mr. Spencer assigns 3 pages of homework for the weekend. How many pages of homework does he assign altogether?

   Mr. Spencer assigns _____ pages of homework altogether.

2. $10 \times 2 =$

3. $16 \times 2 =$

4. $4{,}002 - 3{,}456 =$

5. Look at the Base Ten Blocks. Write the subtraction number sentence shown and the solution.

   _____

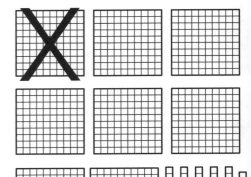

Lesson 152

1. $4{,}345 - 1{,}002 =$

2. Estimate to the nearest hundred.

   $654 + 781$ is about _____ .

3. $11 \times 8 =$

4. Write the number fifty thousand, three hundred three.

   _____

5. A group of 786 people boarded the subway at the first station, another 304 people boarded the subway at the next station, and 297 people boarded the subway at the third station. How many people boarded the subway at all three stations combined?

   _____ people boarded the subway at all three stations combined.

Lesson 153

1. 8,004 − 2,009 =

2. Rosalie has 7 filing cabinets, and each filing cabinet has 12 drawers. How many drawers are there altogether?

    There are _____ drawers altogether.

3. 7,098 − _____ = 4,355

4. 3 x 8 =

5. Circle the number that is greater.

    12,345   21,345

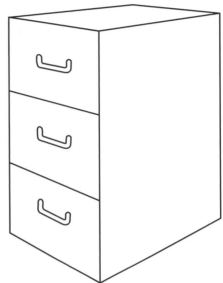

Lesson 154

1. Peggy has 40 balls in a basket. She wants to divide the balls equally between herself and her younger brother. How many balls should each person get?

    Each person should get _____ balls.

2. Use the clues to write a 4-digit number. The digits are 3, 8, 6, and 1. The greatest digit is in the ones place. The smallest digit is in the tens place. The 6 is not in the thousands place.

    The number is _____.

3. 14,567 − 2,345 =

4. 15 x 3 =

5. 50 ÷ 2 =

Lesson 155

1. A small business receives 18 phone calls every day. How many phone calls does the business receive in 5 days?

   The small business receives _____ phone calls.

2. Circle the even number that is least.

   808   916   234   281   307   314

3. 4,345 + 21,345 =

4. 981 − 76 =

5. 44 ÷ 2 =

Lesson 156

1. Ellie and Celia are sisters. They have a doll collection of 28 dolls. They decide to divide the dolls equally. How many dolls will each girl get?

   Ellie and Celia will each get _____ dolls.

2. 12,456 − 9,767 =

3. 31,786 + 2,345 =

4. 50 ÷ 5 =

5. Draw Base Ten Blocks in the box to show the subtraction number sentence 567 − 210 = .

Lesson 157

1. During the back-to-school sale, a store made $13,456 on Saturday and $10,987 on Sunday. How much money did the store make on Saturday and Sunday combined?

   The store made _____ on Saturday and Sunday combined.

2. $25 \div 5 =$

3. $8,867 + 15,654 =$

4. Write the number forty-five thousand, six hundred eighteen.

   _____

5. A newspaper delivers 34,675 papers on Wednesday and 34,567 papers on Saturday. How many newspapers are delivered on Wednesday and Saturday combined?

   _____ papers are delivered on Wednesday and Saturday combined.

Lesson 158

1. Write the number twelve thousand, six hundred seventy-one.

2. $15,786 + 34,566 =$

3. $21,768 - 4,345 =$

4. $3 \times 3 =$

5. Use the clues to write a 4-digit number. The four digits are 6, 5, 4, and 2. There is an odd number in the ones place. The greatest digit belongs in the tens place. The number 2 is not in the hundreds place.

   The number is _____.

Lesson 159

1. 16 x 5 =

2. 66 ÷ 3 =

3. 43 x 2 =

4. Write the number sixty-eight thousand, seven hundred four.

    _____

5. The Children's Museum had a special exhibit for all of the third graders in the city. On Wednesday, 24,654 children visited the museum. On Thursday, 32,876 children visited the museum. On Friday, 19,234 children visited the museum. How many more children visited the museum on Thursday than on Friday?

    _____ more children visited the museum on Thursday than on Friday.

Lesson 160

1. 8,908 + 24,356 =

2. The school has 6,567 textbooks. Of those, 3,456 of the books are math books. The rest are reading books. How many more math books are in the school than reading books?

    There are _____ more math books than reading books.

3. 9,011 – 5,678 =

4. 18 ÷ 3 =

5. Look at the Base Ten Blocks. Write the number shown.

    _____

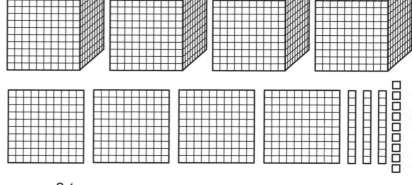

Name _____

Lesson 161

1. A furniture store sends out 32,987 coupons. A total of 2,987 coupons are redeemed for a discount. How many coupons are not redeemed?

   _____ coupons are not redeemed.

2. Estimate to the nearest tens place.

   765 + 433 is about _____ .

3. 34,567 – 21,345 =

4. 44,345 + 6,567 =

5. Use the clues to write a 4-digit number. The number is between 3,000 and 5,000. The 4 digits add up to a sum of 12. There is a 3 in the thousands place. There is a 1 in the tens place. The same digit is in the ones place and the hundreds place.

   The number is _____ .

Lesson 162

1. Patrick played in 18 soccer games during the fall. He scored 3 goals in each game. How many goals did Patrick score in all 18 games?

   Patrick scored a total of _____ goals in all 18 games.

2. 3 x 7 =

3. 16 ÷ 8 =

4. 567 + 678 =

5. Write the number sixty-eight thousand, four hundred eleven.

   _____

Lesson 163

1. Circle the fraction that is equal to $\frac{2}{3}$.

   $\frac{4}{5}$ $\frac{4}{6}$

2. A total of 80 parents attended Back-to-School Night. An equal number of parents visited each of 4 classrooms. How many parents visited each classroom at a time?

   _____ parents visited each classroom at a time.

3. $20 \div 2 =$

4. $15 \times 7 =$

5. Look at the Base Ten Blocks. Write the number shown.

   _____

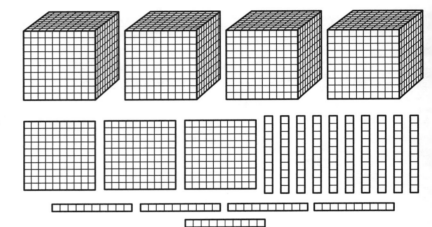

Lesson 164

1. Maddie is trying to figure out her grandmother's age at a particular time. She knows that her grandmother was born in 1924. How old is Maddie's grandmother in the year 2003?

   Maddie's grandmother is _____ years old in the year 2003.

2. $43,567 + 8,685 =$

3. $6,577 - \rule{2cm}{0.4pt} = 4,003$

4. $9 \times \rule{1.5cm}{0.4pt} = 63$

5. Write the number in standard form. $50,000 + 4,000 + 2$

   _____

Lesson 165

1. Circle the even number that is greater than 2,500 but less than 3,000.

   2,456   2,987   3,040   2,424   2,978   2,681

2. $6 \times$ _____ $= 36$

3. A group of 4 students is writing a report about sharks. They find a total of 40 Web sites about sharks. They each plan to look at an equal number of Web sites and then discuss the information they find. How many Web sites will each student look at?

   Each student will look at _____ Web sites.

4. $34{,}876 -$ _____ $= 24{,}345$

5. $14 \times 8 =$

Lesson 166

1. Write the numbers in order from least to greatest.

   18,767   19,008   21,345   18,977   20,333

   _____

2. $5{,}098 +$ _____ $= 13{,}876$

3. $2 \times$ _____ $= 18$

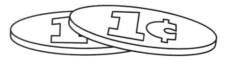

4. $72 \div 8 =$

5. David's third-grade class collected pennies all year. At the end of the year, they had collected a total of 67,897 pennies. They spent 54,876 pennies to help pay for a class field trip. They gave the rest of the money to the library to buy books. How many pennies did the third graders give to the library?

   The third graders gave _____ pennies to the library.

Lesson 167

1. There are 3 vases in the living room. Each vase is filled with 11 flowers. How many flowers are there in all?

   There are _____ flowers in all.

2. $42 \div 2 =$

3. $8 \times 9 =$

4. $45,767 - \text{_____} = 29,008$

5. Draw Base Ten Blocks in the box to show 909.

Lesson 168

1. Circle the fraction that is equal to $\frac{5}{8}$.

   $\frac{10}{16}$ $\qquad$ $\frac{12}{16}$

2. There are 20 students in Mr. Hanover's class. Half of Mr. Hanover's students wear glasses or contacts. How many of Mr. Hanover's students do not wear glasses or contacts?

   _____ of Mr. Hanover's students do not wear glasses or contacts.

3. $20 \times 3 =$

4. $36 \div 3 =$

5. Write the number two hundred thousand, five.

   _____

Lesson 169

1.　8,098 + 3,456 =

2.　$7 \times$ _____ = 63

3.　12 ÷ 6 =

4.　Circle the odd number between 4,000 and 4,500.

　　3,998　4,001　4,448　4,716

5.　A science teacher needs each of his students to wear a pair of gloves in order to participate in an experiment. How many individual gloves does the science teacher need so that 9 students may participate in the experiment?

　　The science teacher needs _____ individual gloves for 9 students.

Lesson 170

1.　24 ÷ 4 =

2.　7,008 − _____ = 567

3.　11 x 10 =

4.　Pamela spends $34.80 on back-to-school supplies and $87.65 on back-to-school clothes. How much money does Pamela spend in all?

　　Pamela spends _____ in all.

5.　Look at the Base Ten Blocks. Write the number shown.

　　_____

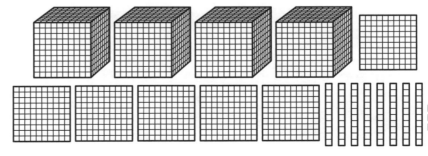

Lesson 171

1. Write the missing number to complete the pattern.

   2, 4, 8, _____, 32

2. Estimate to the nearest ten.

   704 – 456 is about _____ .

3. Estimate to the nearest hundred.

   996 + 452 is about _____ .

4. 9,087 – 4,567 =

5. Mrs. Hannon is planning a class project using clay. She buys a total of 12 packages of clay. Each package of clay contains 6 pieces. How many pieces of clay are there in all 12 packages combined?

   There are _____ pieces of clay in all 12 packages combined.

Lesson 172

1. Write the missing letters to complete the pattern.

   A, A, Z, F, F, X, K, K, _____, _____, P, T

2. 3,456 + 23,432 =

3. 8 x 11 =

4. 9 x 15 =

5. The postal carrier can deliver 21 letters every 5 minutes. How many letters can she deliver in 30 minutes?

   The postal carrier can deliver _____ letters in 30 minutes.

Lesson 173

1. $7 \times 8 =$

2. $34{,}546 - 2{,}001 =$

3. The stadium sold 45,768 tickets for the first game and 77,002 tickets for the second game. How many tickets did the stadium sell for both games combined?

   The stadium sold _____ tickets for both games combined.

4. $16 \times 7 =$

5. Draw the missing shapes to complete the pattern.

Lesson 174

1. Fill in the missing numbers to complete the pattern.

   333, 336, _____, 342, 345, _____

2. $42 \times 3 =$

3. $54{,}675 - 1{,}118 =$

4. $7{,}008 + 21{,}456 =$

5. Jerry was born in 1972. When he celebrated his birthday on February 8, 2002, what birthday was he celebrating?

   Jerry was celebrating his _____th birthday.

Lesson 175

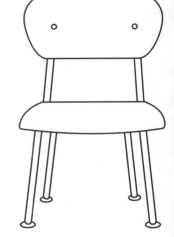

1. There are 8 tables in the art room. Each table has 8 chairs surrounding it. How many chairs are around all 8 tables?

    There are _____ chairs around all 8 tables.

2. $64 \div 4 =$

3. $19,765 - 14,786 =$

4. $9 \times 2 =$

5. Draw the missing lines to complete the pattern.

Lesson 176

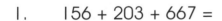

1. $156 + 203 + 667 =$

2. $904 - 78 =$

3. $17 \times 7 =$

4. The football team has 20 bags of practice footballs. There are 8 footballs in each bag. How many footballs are in all 20 bags?

    There are _____ footballs in all 20 bags.

5. Fill in the missing numbers to complete the pattern.

    22, 44, 88, _____, _____, 704

Lesson 177

1. $91 + 114 + 345 =$

2. Fill in the blank with >, <, or = to make the number sentence true.

   4,567 _____ 3,564

3. $78,908 - 65,898 =$

4. $765 + \text{\_\_\_\_\_} + 201 = 1,567$

5. Samantha bought balloons for a carnival. She has 708 red balloons, 644 blue balloons, 334 yellow balloons. How many more red balloons than yellow balloons does Samantha have?

   Samantha has _____ more red balloons than yellow balloons.

Lesson 178

1. Fill in the blank with <, >, or = to make the number sentence true.

   23,456 _____ 21,564

2. $89,004 + 56,567 =$

3. $17,897 - \text{_____} = 11,987$

4. $16 \times 4 =$

5. $21 \div 3 =$

Lesson 179

1. 65,987 + _____ = 74,989

2. 6 x 8 =

3. 15,675 – _____ = 12,555

4. There are 18 walls in the museum. There are 8 paintings on each wall.
    How many paintings are on all 18 walls?

    There are _____ paintings on all 18 walls.

5. Round the number to the nearest hundred. 5,678

    _____

Lesson 180

1. Amanda is looking up new words from the book she is reading. On
    each page of her book, she finds 4 words that she needs to look up.
    Her book is 35 pages long. How many words does Amanda look up?

    Amanda looks up _____ words.

2. 721 + 68 – 496 =

3. 9 ÷ 3 =

4. 82 ÷ 2 =

5. Solve each number sentence.
    Then, fill in the blank with <, >, or =
    to make the number sentence true.

    33 + 18 – 4 _____ 44 + 21 – 2

    _____ _____ _____

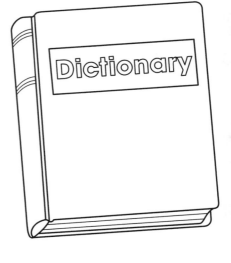

Answer Key: Lessons 1–20

Lesson 1
1. fifteenth
2. 3
3. 133
4. 33 – 17 = 16; picture drawn; 16
5. 443

Lesson 2
1. 1,533
2. 35
3. 3
4. 11
5. Sue

Lesson 3
1. 947
2. 3,865
3. 169
4. $0.85 + $1.35 = $2.20; $2.20
5. 788

Lesson 4
1. $2.25 – $0.75 = $1.50; $1.50
2. 1,601
3. 239
4. 55
5. 4,341

Lesson 5
1. 24
2. 9,614
3. 749
4. 134
5.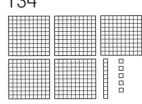

Lesson 6
1. 5,000
2. 5,003
3. 4,574
4. 53
5. 9 + 9 (or 9 x 2) = 18; picture drawn; 18

Lesson 7
1. 123, 343, 709, 765, 788
2. 21
3. 123
4. 643
5. 1,309

Lesson 8
1. 898, 756, 675, 223, 201
2. 24
3. 321
4. 3,345
5. 430

Lesson 9
1. 5,048
2. 110, 708, 801, 810, 811
3. 4, 3, 6
4. 720
5. 359

Lesson 10
1. 7,849
2. nineteenth
3. 160
4. 904
5. 221 – 118 = 103; 103

Lesson 11
1. 28
2. 11
3. 4
4. 5
5. 10

Lesson 12
1. 12; 18; 21
2. 39
3. 44
4. 7
5. 29

Lesson 13
1. 6
2. 18
3. Green; Orange
4. 10
5. 600

Lesson 14
1. 20
2. 30
3. 143
4. 10
5. ⬡; △

Lesson 15
1. 121
2. 5
3. 4
4. 69
5. 15 – 3 = 12 picture drawn

Lesson 16
1. 12
2. 294
3. 350
4. V; R; R
5. 33

Lesson 17
1. 45
2. 60
3. 16
4. 580
5. 9 x 4 = 36 picture drawn

Lesson 18
1. 12
2. 791
3. 13
4. 6
5. 27 – 14 = 13; 13

Lesson 19
1. 8
2. 3
3. 374
4. 34
5. 94; 106

Lesson 20
1. 0
2. 438
3. 55
4. 300
5. ↑↑

Daily Math Warm-Ups Grade 3

Answer Key: Lessons 21–42

Lesson 21
1. 4
2. 189
3. 15
4. 20
5. 60; 60; 90

Lesson 22
1. 8
2. 4
3. 328
4. 30
5. 288

Lesson 23
1. 50; 70; 90
2. 10
3. 908
4. 111
5. 25

Lesson 24
1. 64
2. 15
3. 23
4. 325
5. 125

Lesson 25
1. 62
2. 36
3. 22
4. 116
5. 145

Lesson 26
1. 211
2. 36
3. 30
4. 35
5. 100; 100; 200

Lesson 27
1. 36
2. 573
3. 23
4. 18
5. 28

Lesson 28
1. 36
2. 504
3. 123
4. 16
5. 67

Lesson 29
1. 150
2. 700
3. 25
4. 10
5. 34

Lesson 30
1. 4
2. 62
3. 266
4. 616
5. 28

Lesson 31
1. 20
2. 361
3. 9
4. 36
5. 6 x 8 = 48; 48

Lesson 32
1. 37
2. 505
3. 372
4. 72
5. 3

Lesson 33
1. 54
2. 34
3. 48
4. 40
5. 16 + 20 + 12 = 48 letters

Lesson 34
1. 8
2. 37
3. 142
4. 618
5. $0.75

Lesson 35
1. 24
2. 54
3. 41
4. 155
5. 20

Lesson 36
1. 168
2. 352
3. 49
4. 723
5. 50

Lesson 37
1. 10
2. 63
3. 12
4. 33
5. 12

Lesson 38
1. 14
2. 556
3. 64
4. 209
5. 9

Lesson 39
1. 27
2. 339
3. 43
4. 90
5. 171

Lesson 40
1. 36
2. 63
3. 12
4. 60
5.

Lesson 41
1. B
2. 259
3. 629
4. 270
5. 522

Lesson 42
1. 30
2. 375; 275
3. 100
4. 212
5. 81

Answer Key: Lessons 43–63

Lesson 43
1. 6
2. 396
3. 56
4. 90
5. ◯ ; ◯

Lesson 44
1. D
2. 14
3. 12
4. 72
5. 15

Lesson 45
1. 16
2. 126
3. 250
4. 24
5. K; N; Z

Lesson 46
1. 81
2. B
3. 21
4. 28
5. 28

Lesson 47
1. 28
2. C
3. 28
4. 368
5. 9

Lesson 48
1. ▯ ; ▭
2. 12
3. 389
4. 64
5. 14

Lesson 49
1. 5 minutes;
   7 minutes
2. 37
3. 64
4. 500
5. 100

Lesson 50
1. 221
2. 73; 75
3. 59
4. 52
5. 160

Lesson 51
1. 206
2. A
3. 56
4. 548
5. 21

Lesson 52
1. <
2. 980
3. 84
4. 965
5. 110

Lesson 53
1. 249
2. 1,357
3. 42
4. 16
5. D

Lesson 54
1. 18
2. 1,000
3. 72
4. 50
5. B

Lesson 55
1. 10
2. 800
3. <
4. 24
5. 5,000

Lesson 56
1. 700
2. 34
3. 681
4. 8
5. 40

Lesson 57
1. 98
2. 5 x 7 = 35
3. 77
4. 8,000
5. 800

Lesson 58
1. 24
2. 887
3. 0
4. 128
5. 27 – 5 = 22

Lesson 59
1. 9 x 8 = 72
2. 177
3. 3,781
4. 90
5. 18

Lesson 60
1. <
2. 18
3. 66
4. 16 hats drawn
   in 4 groups of 4
5. 10

Lesson 61
1. 9
2. 249
3. 12
4. 12
5.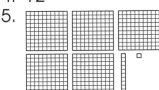

Lesson 62
1. >
2. 210; 550
3. 5
4. 7,547
5. 8

Lesson 63
1. 133, 288, 301,
   310, 425
2. 5,766
3. 6,000 + 700 +
   80 + 9
4. 118
5. 100

Daily Math Warm-Ups Grade 3

Answer Key: Lessons 64–80

Lesson 64
1. two thousand three hundred thirteen
2. 25
3. 2
4. 15
5. 3,408

Lesson 65
1. >
2. 49
3. 0
4. 7
5. 901, 806, 786, 705, 449, 75

Lesson 66
1. 6
2. 23
3. 2,002
4. 14
5. $\frac{7}{8}$

Lesson 67
1. 6,233
2. 84
3. 4,054; 1,298
4. 6
5. 7,257

Lesson 68
1. 118
2. 5,284
3. 5,833
4. 64
5. 83

Lesson 69
1. 56
2. 72
3. 11,887
4. 12
5.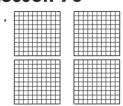

Lesson 70
1.
2. 9
3. 20
4. 8,765; 8,310; 8,011; 4,323; 2,132
5. 10

Lesson 71
1. 20
2. 29
3. 5,999
4. 77
5. octagon; 8 angles

Lesson 72
1. 85
2. 4
3. 31
4. 42
5. 12

Lesson 73
1. 8
2. 40
3. 8
4. 6
5. rectangular prism; sphere; cone

Lesson 74
1. (hexagon)
2. 25
3. 9
4. 3
5. 492

Lesson 75
1. 79
2. 4,615
3. 18
4. 697
5. 3

Lesson 76
1. 7,101
2. 9
3. 136
4. 13
5. the first and last figures circled

Lesson 77
1. 100
2. 6,774
3. 38
4. 16
5.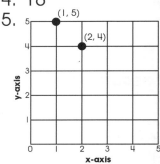

Lesson 78
1. 8,210
2. 16
3. 37
4. 56
5. (star) ; (light bulb)

Lesson 79
1. 1,300
2. 7
3. 183
4. 6,378
5. (parallelogram)

Lesson 80
1. 48
2. 88
3. 6,911
4. 15
5. flip

Answer Key: Lessons 81–101

Lesson 81
1.

2. 11,436
3. 8
4. 5
5. 11

Lesson 82
1. 2
2. 15
3. 8
4. 2,565
5.

Lesson 83
1. sphere
2. 5
3. 7,812
4. 838
5. 8,568

Lesson 84
1. 9
2. 16
3. 30
4. 593
5. G

Lesson 85
1. 744
2. 10,221
3. 11
4. 1,026
5. cube

Lesson 86
1. 2
2. 1,114
3. 12,683
4. 10
5. triangle; rectangle; circle

Lesson 87
1. 84
2. 34
3. 2
4. 1,736
5. rectangle

Lesson 88
1. 12
2. 5
3. 2,637
4. 22
5. congruent triangle drawn

Lesson 89
1. 77
2. 8,773
3. 199
4. 244
5. congruent hexagon drawn

Lesson 90
1. 96
2. 1,671
3. 9
4. 323
5. similar

Lesson 91
1. 12
2. 28
3. 1,778
4. 11
5. pictures will vary

Lesson 92
1. 14
2. 5
3. 13,332
4. 228
5. pyramid

Lesson 93
1. 5,334
2. 102
3. 24
4. 6
5. slide

Lesson 94
1. 40
2. 688
3. 379
4. 48
5. 6; 12

Lesson 95
1. 5
2. 101
3. 32
4. 11
5. 8

Lesson 96
1. 42
2. 228
3. 63
4. 4
5. cylinder

Lesson 97
1. 4
2. 660
3. 6,891
4. 4
5. the first and last squares

Lesson 98
1. 46
2. 54
3. 6
4. 136
5. square; square drawn

Lesson 99
1. 851
2. 4
3. 5
4. 82
5. 0

Lesson 100
1. 16
2. 1,330
3. 9
4. 10
5. sphere circled

Lesson 101
1. 21
2. 461
3. 3
4. 1,092
5. 8

 Daily Math Warm-Ups Grade 3

Answer Key: Lessons 102–122

Lesson 102
1. feet
2. 64
3. 7
4. 9
5. 1,478

Lesson 103
1. 740
2.
3. 6,277
4. 125
5. 3

Lesson 104
1. 41
2. 55
3. 126
4. 10
5. 12

Lesson 105
1. 1,292
2. 0
3. 465
4. 5
5. 7

Lesson 106
1. 5
2. 1,003
3. 36
4. 12
5. 27

Lesson 107
1. 54
2. 5 gallons
3. 6,118
4. 727
5. 12

Lesson 108
1. 32
2. 25
3. 2
4. 114
5. 8

Lesson 109
1. 5,350
2. 36
3. 5,118
4. 215
5.

Lesson 110
1. 48
2. cone
3. 9
4. 81
5. 6,887

Lesson 111
1. 5
2. 99
3. 2,391
4. 124
5. 1:30

Lesson 112
1. 9
2. 24
3. 4
4. 662
5. 1 cup

Lesson 113
1. 71
2. 72
3. 1,179
4. 2
5.

Lesson 114
1. 6
2. 5,006
3. 10
4. 9,242
5. 32

Lesson 115
1. 149
2. 231
3. 767
4. 55
5. 64

Lesson 116
1. 5
2. 3
3. 6,477
4. 1,986
5. 85

Lesson 117
1. 60
2. 11,630
3. 1,723
4. 2
5. 2

Lesson 118
1. 464
2. 2,244
3. 24
4. 7
5. 5 kilograms

Lesson 119
1. 4,355
2. 3,848
3. 1,716
4. 80
5. 4

Lesson 120
1. 60
2. 8
3. 72
4. 100
5. 9:35

Lesson 121
1. 1,747
2. 16,110
3. 215
4. 8
5. $\frac{20}{100}$

Lesson 122
1. 12
2. 10,260
3. 243
4. 35
5. 3,717

Answer Key: Lessons 123–143

Lesson 123
1. 103
2. 971
3. $36.92
4. 100,645
5. 876, 801, 717, 701, 544

Lesson 124
1. 108
2. 117, 201, 208, 333, 359
3. 10
4. 10,990
5. 2,164

Lesson 125
1. 60
2. 202; 404
3. 4
4. 105
5. $\frac{7}{8}$ shaded

Lesson 126
1. 880, 818, 811, 808, 756, 709
2. 548
3. 64
4. 21,018
5.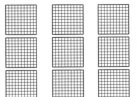

Lesson 127
1. $50.93
2. 677; 413
3. 149
4. 44
5. 9

Lesson 128
1. $\frac{2}{4}$
2. 20
3. 53
4. 8,537
5. 15,302

Lesson 129
1. 126
2. 568, 515, 505, 414, 123
3. 6
4. 3,445
5. 699 – 287 = 412

Lesson 130
1. $55.00
2. 5,457
3. 132
4. 200,685
5. X01; 3,X56; 1,X98

Lesson 131
1. 48
2. 21
3. 81
4. 8,755
5. June

Lesson 132
1. 10
2. 71
3. 56
4. 8
5. 30

Lesson 133
1. 18
2. 877
3. 1,015
4. 54
5. Thursday

Lesson 134
1. 302
2. 3
3. 96
4. 10
5. 64

Lesson 135
1. 600
2. 1
3. 2,531
4. 121
5. 8

Lesson 136
1. 13,552
2. 40
3. 422
4. 16
5. A

Lesson 137
1. 72
2. 1,109
3. 636
4. 72
5. 144

Lesson 138
1. 29
2. 100
3. 144
4. 1,052
5. 75

Lesson 139
1. 40
2. 20,556
3. 2,794
4. 4,652
5. 12

Lesson 140
1. 120
2. 29,686
3. 99
4. 10
5. 200

Lesson 141
1. 376
2. 37,533
3. 380; 320
4. 80
5. 45

Lesson 142
1. 1,324
2. 748
3. 1,000
4. 36
5. G

Lesson 143
1. 383
2. 20
3. 110
4. 6
5. 213 and 875 circled

Answer Key: Lessons 144–164

Lesson 144
1. 90
2. 81
3.
4. 7,311
5. 11

Lesson 145
1. 1,500
2. $34.26
3. 4,531
4. 4
5. 56; 50; 48

Lesson 146
1. 1,340
2. 26
3. 3
4. 8
5. quarter

Lesson 147
1. 740
2. 400
3. 42
4. 375; 275; 225
5. 9

Lesson 148
1. 36
2. 644
3. 1,447
4. 12,023
5. = ; ⊥

Lesson 149
1. 3,000
2. 30
3. 6
4. C; C; F
5. 24

Lesson 150
1. 18
2. 200
3. 1,178
4. 1,000
5. △ ; ▽

Lesson 151
1. 51
2. 20
3. 32
4. 546
5. 856 − 122 = 734

Lesson 152
1. 3,343
2. 1,500
3. 88
4. 50,303
5. 1,387

Lesson 153
1. 5,995
2. 84
3. 2,743
4. 24
5. 21,343

Lesson 154
1. 20
2. 3,618
3. 12,222
4. 45
5. 25

Lesson 155
1. 90
2. 234
3. 25,690
4. 905
5. 22

Lesson 156
1. 14
2. 2,689
3. 34,131
4. 10
5.

Lesson 157
1. $24,443
2. 5
3. 24,521
4. 45,618
5. 69,242

Lesson 158
1. 12,671
2. 50,352
3. 17,423
4. 9
5. 2,465

Lesson 159
1. 80
2. 22
3. 86
4. 68,704
5. 13,642

Lesson 160
1. 33,264
2. 3,111
3. 3,333
4. 6
5. 4,439

Lesson 161
1. 30,000
2. 1,200
3. 13,222
4. 50,912
5. 3,414

Lesson 162
1. 54
2. 21
3. 2
4. 1,245
5. 68,411

Lesson 163
1. $\frac{4}{6}$
2. 20
3. 10
4. 105
5. 4,450

Lesson 164
1. 79
2. 52,252
3. 2,574
4. 7
5. 54,002

Answer Key: Lessons 165–180

Lesson 165
1. 2,978
2. 6
3. 10
4. 10,531
5. 112

Lesson 166
1. 18,767; 18,977; 19,008; 20,333; 21,345
2. 8,778
3. 9
4. 9
5. 13,021

Lesson 167
1. 33
2. 21
3. 72
4. 16,759
5.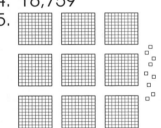

Lesson 168
1. $\dfrac{10}{16}$
2. 10
3. 60
4. 12
5. 200,005

Lesson 169
1. 11,554
2. 9
3. 2
4. 4,001
5. 18

Lesson 170
1. 6
2. 6,441
3. 110
4. $122.45
5. 4,683

Lesson 171
1. 16
2. 240
3. 1,500
4. 4,520
5. 72

Lesson 172
1. V; P
2. 26,888
3. 88
4. 135
5. 126

Lesson 173
1. 56
2. 32,545
3. 122,770
4. 112
5. ▭ ; ◯

Lesson 174
1. 339; 348
2. 126
3. 53,557
4. 28,464
5. 30th

Lesson 175
1. 64
2. 16
3. 4,979
4. 18
5. ⊥ ; =

Lesson 176
1. 1,026
2. 826
3. 119
4. 160
5. 176; 352

Lesson 177
1. 550
2. >
3. 13,010
4. 601
5. 374

Lesson 178
1. >
2. 145,571
3. 5,910
4. 64
5. 7

Lesson 179
1. 9,002
2. 48
3. 3,120
4. 144
5. 5,700

Lesson 180
1. 140
2. 293
3. 3
4. 41
5. <; 47 < 63

Assessment 1 (Lessons 1–10)

Name _____

1. 37 + 41 =

A. 77
B. 78
C. 71
D. 87

2. 271 – 198 =

A. 71
B. 73
C. 74
D. 69

3. 505 + 404 =

A. 101
B. 1,001
C. 99
D. 909

4. What is the number in standard form?

6,000 + 90 + 2

A. 6,992
B. 6,902
C. 6,092
D. 6,009

5. Put the numbers in order from greatest to least.

231, 201, 244, 378, 301

A. 378, 301, 244, 231, 201
B. 378, 244, 301, 201, 231
C. 301, 244, 378, 201, 231
D. 201, 231, 244, 301, 378

6. What is this number in written form?

5,675

A. five thousand six hundred seventy-five
B. five thousand six hundred seventy
C. six hundred seventy-five thousand, five
D. five hundred seventy-five

7. What number do the Base Ten Blocks show?

A. 235
B. 325
C. 305
D. 3,025

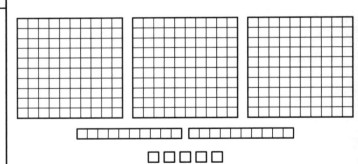

8. Joe plants 89 trees along a busy highway on Saturday. On Sunday, he plants 14 more trees than he plants on Saturday. How many trees does Joe plant on Sunday.

A. 75
B. 113
C. 103
D. 33

Assessment 2 (Lessons 11–20)

Name _____

1. $79 - 42 =$

A. 40
B. 41
C. 37
D. 38

2. Which lines are missing in the pattern?

A.

B.

C.

D.

3. $12 + \underline{\hspace{1cm}} = 31$

A. 22
B. 11
C. 19
D. 21

4. $39 - 17 =$

A. 2
B. 25
C. 24
D. 22

5. Write the missing numbers to complete the pattern.

425, 400, _____, 350, 325, _____

A. 375, 300
B. 300, 350
C. 250, 275
D. 325, 450

6. $554 - 127 =$

A. 427
B. 417
C. 437
D. 681

7. $138 - 119 =$

A. 21
B. 19
C. 27
D. 91

8. Molly travels a distance of 424 miles Monday and 555 miles Tuesday. How many miles does Molly travel in all?

A. 919
B. 909
C. 979
D. 879

Assessment 3 (Lessons 21–30)

Name _____

1. 3 x 2 =

A. 5
B. 6
C. 4
D. 8

2. 493 – 55 =

A. 425
B. 422
C. 548
D. 438

3. 240 + 238 =

A. 212
B. 428
C. 458
D. 478

4. 33 – 9 =

A. 44
B. 42
C. 24
D. 26

5. Round each number to the nearest tens place.

33   47   55

A. 20, 50, 50
B. 30, 50, 50
C. 30, 50, 60
D. 35, 50, 55

Use the bar graph to answer questions 6 and 7.

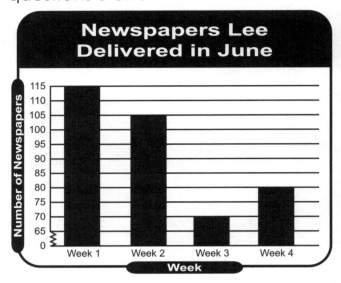

6. How many newspapers did Lee deliver during all of June?

A. 370
B. 355
C. 305
D. 345

7. How many more newspapers did Lee deliver during week 2 than during week 3?

A. 18
B. 15
C. 35
D. 5

8. Round each number to the nearest hundreds place.
    155   444   201

A. 200, 500, 200
B. 100, 200, 300
C. 200, 400, 250
D. 200, 400, 200

Assessment 4 (Lessons 31–40)

Name _____

1. 216 − 87 =

  A. 119
  B. 303
  C. 129
  D. 313

2. 41 + 10 − 5 =

  A. 39
  B. 51
  C. 46
  D. 45

3. 7 x 8 =

  A. 64
  B. 42
  C. 49
  D. 56

4. 56 − 49 =

  A. 7
  B. 8
  C. 105
  D. 12

5. A group of 8 children are taking piano lessons. They each practice piano 2 hours a day. How many hours do all 8 children practice?

  A. 12
  B. 24
  C. 16
  D. 10

Use the table to answer questions 6 and 7.

Cans Collected

Family	Number of Cans
Owen	212
Nalle	199
Smith	103
Bentley	56

6. How many cans were collected in all?

  A. 517
  B. 570
  C. 527
  D. 455

7. How many more cans did the Owen and Smith families collect than the Nalle and Bentley families?

  A. 500
  B. 60
  C. 55
  D. 47

8. Laura spun a blue and green spinner 23 times. It landed on green 11 times. How many times did it land on blue?

  A. 12
  B. 14
  C. 13
  D. 11

Assessment 5 (Lessons 41–50)

Name _____

1. Ms. Hall orders 3 books for each of her third graders. She has 11 third graders in her class. How many books does Ms. Hall order for all 11 third graders?

   A. 33
   B. 13
   C. 30
   D. 23

2. Estimate.

   55 + 71 is about _____ .

   A. 125
   B. 130
   C. 113
   D. 103

3. 17 + 8 − 12 =

   A. 15
   B. 12
   C. 13
   D. 18

4. 52 − 14 =

   A. 37
   B. 66
   C. 68
   D. 38

5. 784 + 671 =

   A. 1,455
   B. 1,050
   C. 1,500
   D. 1,045

6. 701 + 68 =

   A. 769
   B. 633
   C. 623
   D. 709

7. Circle the statement below that best describes what is happening in the pattern.

   5, 15, 10, 20, 15, 25, 20, 30, 25

   A. 5 is subtracted from every number.
   B. 5 is subtracted. Then, 5 is added.
   C. 10 is added. Then, 5 is subtracted.
   D. 6 is subtracted. Then, 5 is added.

8. Drew has 18 buttons in a box. Of those, 9 buttons are purple, 6 buttons are black, 2 buttons are white, and 1 button is yellow. If Drew selects a button at random, what color is it most likely to be?

   A. yellow
   B. white
   C. purple
   D. black

Assessment 6 (Lessons 51–60)

Name _____

1. Which symbol will make the number sentence true?

   3,044 _____ 1,307

   A. >
   B. <
   C. =

2. Estimate to the nearest hundred. 465 + 671 is about _____ .

   A.   200
   B. 1,250
   C. 1,100
   D. 1,200

3. Which number sentence does the picture show?

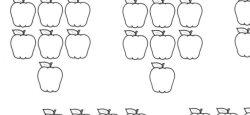

   A. 7 x 4 =
   B. 7 + 5 =
   C. 5 x 7 =
   D. 5 + 5 + 5 =

4. 10 x 10 =

   A.   90
   B. 100
   C.   85
   D.   10

5. Which number sentence does the picture show?

   A. 9 – 3 =
   B. 9 + 3 =
   C. 9 ÷ 3 =
   D. 9 x 3 =

6. Which symbol will make the number sentence true?

   799 _____ 641

   A. >
   B. <
   C. =

7. There are 12 people in Albert's class. Half of the students have brown eyes and half have blue eyes. How many students with brown eyes are in Albert's class?

   A. 5
   B. 4
   C. 8
   D. 6

8. 584 + 901 =

   A.   400
   B. 1,041
   C. 1,444
   D. 1,485

Assessment 7 (Lessons 61–70)

Name _____

1. What number do the Base Ten Blocks show?

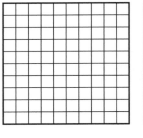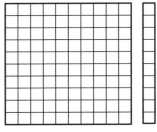

A. 207
B. 217
C. 270
D. 277

2. What is the number in standard form?

two thousand nine hundred sixteen

A. 2,619
B. 2,916
C. 2,096
D. 2,900

3. What is the number in expanded form? 5,789

A. 500 + 700 + 80 + 9
B. 5,000 + 780 + 9
C. 5,000 + 700 + 80 + 9
D. 5,000 + 700 + 88 + 1

4. 9 x 6 =

A. 46
B. 45
C. 15
D. 54

5. Circle the answer choice that shows $\frac{1}{2}$ of the circles shaded.

A.

B.

C.

D.

6. Which symbol will make the number sentence true?

2,001 _____ 2,011

A. >
B. <
C. =

7. A baker decorates 3 cakes with 7 flowers each. How many flowers does she use for all 3 cakes?

A. 18
B. 17
C. 21
D. 20

8. Put the numbers in order from greatest to least.

2,564   1,276   2,010   3,767   2,013

A. 1,276; 2,010; 2,013; 2,564; 3,767
B. 2,564; 2,013, 2,010, 3,767; 1,276
C. 3,767; 2,013; 2,564; 2,010; 1,276
D. 3,767; 2,564; 2,013; 2,010, 1,276

Assessment 8 (Lessons 71–80)

Name _____

1. Courtney bicycles 9 miles every day for 11 days. How many miles does she bicycle in all 11 days combined?

   A. 98
   B. 20
   C. 99
   D. 75

2. 9,088 + 2,453 =

   A. 11,451
   B. 11,504
   C. 11,541
   D. 6,635

3. 234 – _____ = 86

   A. 151
   B. 108
   C. 320
   D. 148

4. Circle the letter beside the shape being described:
   The shape is three-dimensional. Some of its faces are triangles. Its base is a square.

   A.   B.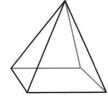

   C. 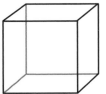 D.

5. The second graders at Lynnwood Elementary School organize a canned food drive. They collect 2,098 cans 1 week and 3,015 cans the next week. How many more cans do the students collect during the second week?

   A. 5,113
   B. 970
   C. 917
   D. 5,131

6. Which of the answer choices shows a point on (4,3)?

   A. A
   B. B
   C. C
   D. D

   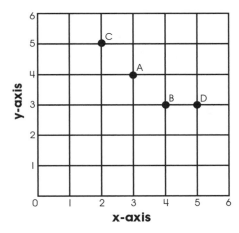

7. How many edges does a rectangular prism have?

   A. 12
   B. 8
   C. 6
   D. 4

   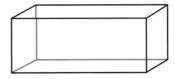

8. 9 x 9 =

   A. 81
   B. 18
   C. 72
   D. 78

Assessment 9 (Lessons 81–90)

Name _____

1. Look at the 4 objects. Circle the triangle that has 3 sides that are the same length.

A.

B.

C.

D.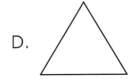

2. Circle the letter that shows a line of symmetry.

A.

B.

C.

D.

3. Look at the shapes below. Circle the word or words that best describe the relationship between the shapes.

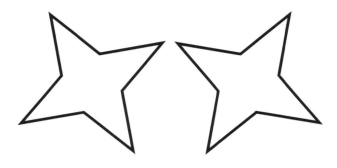

A. congruent
B. different
C. similar
D. none of the above

4. This shape is three-dimensional. It has 1 curved side and 2 flat faces. Which shape is it?

A. cube
B. cylinder
C. sphere
D. rectangular prism

5. A group of 64 people sign up for aerobics at the community center. The teacher wants to break the group into 8 equal classes. How many people will be in each aerobics class?

A. 70
B. 12
C. 8
D. 6

6. $4 \times \underline{\hspace{1cm}} = 16$

A. 5
B. 4
C. 6
D. 12

7. $8{,}098 + 3{,}872 =$

A. 11,970
B. 11,907
C. 11,790
D. 7,678

8. $876 - \underline{\hspace{1cm}} = 201$

A. 675
B. 555
C. 605
D. 576

Assessment 10 (Lessons 91–100)

Name _____

1. Which leaf has a line of symmetry?

A. 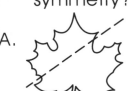   B.

C.    D.

2. What is the name of this shape?

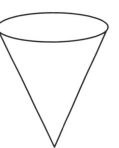

A. cylinder
B. cone
C. cube
D. rectangular prism

3. $56 \div$ _____ $= 8$

A. 5
B. 7
C. 9
D. 4

4. $67 +$ _____ $- 18 = 76$

A. 26
B. 11
C. 25
D. 27

5. Which 2 shapes show a flip?

A.   B.

C. ○ ◯   D. ▷◁

6. Near the end of the school year, there are 77 jackets in the Lost and Found. Later, 38 children visit the Lost and Found and find their jackets. On the last day of school, during playground cleanup, 7 more jackets are turned in. How many jackets are in the Lost and Found box now?

A. 37
B. 39
C. 46
D. 45

7. $12 \times 8 =$

A. 96
B. 95
C. 88
D. 76

8. $40 \div 4 =$

A. 10
B. 5
C. 12
D. 6

Assessment 11 (Lessons 101–110)

Name _____

1. Sean had 138 points and Jakob had 167 points. How many more points did Jakob have than Sean?

   A. 38 points
   B. 27 points
   C. 31 points
   D. 29 points

2. About how much does a basketball weigh?

   A. 5 pounds
   B. 5 ounces
   C. 5 inches
   D. 5 grams

3. How long is the pencil?

   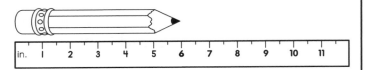

   A. 4 inches
   B. 6 inches
   C. 8 inches
   D. 6 feet

4. How many feet long is the box?

   1 foot

   3 feet

   A. 1 feet
   B. 2 feet
   C. 3 feet
   D. 4 feet

5. What is the perimeter of the shape?

   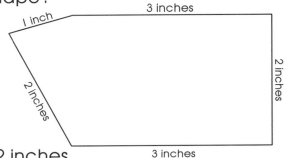

   A. 12 inches
   B. 10 inches
   C. 11 inches
   D. 15 inches

6. What is the perimeter of the square?

   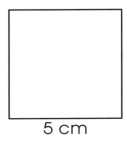

   5 cm

   A. 8 centimeters
   B. 15 centimeters
   C. 20 centimeters
   D. 25 centimeters

7. $24 \div 6 =$

   A. 4
   B. 6
   C. 2
   D. 3

8. $2,329 - 692 =$

   A. 1,621
   B. 1,577
   C. 1,637
   D. 3,021

Assessment 12 (Lessons 111–120)   Name _____

1. Find the volume of the rectangular prism.

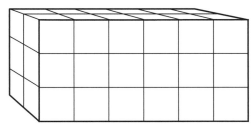

A. 36 cubic units
B. 28 cubic units
C. 34 cubic units
D. 32 cubic units

2. Look at the clock. What time will it be in 3 hours and 15 minutes?

A. 3:25
B. 3:30
C. 3:45
D. 12:45

3. What is the best unit of measure to find the length of a pen?

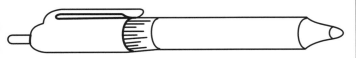

A. ounces
B. pounds
C. feet
D. inches

4. 2,567 + 4,354 =

A. 6,921
B. 5,930
C. 6,904
D. 5,923

5. What temperature is shown on the thermometer?

A. 67° F
B. 60° F
C. 76° F
D. 55° F

6. What is the area of the rectangle?

4 units
7 units

A. 11 square units
B. 22 square units
C. 16 square units
D. 28 square units

7. 5,467 + 1,232 − 89 =

A. 7,444
B. 6,610
C. 6,666
D. 7,890

8. 16 ÷ 2 =

A. 4
B. 16
C. 12
D. 8

Assessment 13 (Lessons 121–130)

Name _____

1. 7 x 7 =

   A. 49
   B. 56
   C. 42
   D. 77

2. What is the number in standard form?

   nineteen thousand, six hundred seven

   A. 19,760
   B. 19,670
   C. 19,607
   D. 19,603

3. Put the numbers in order from least to greatest.

   799, 401, 798, 708, 807

   A. 807; 799; 798; 708; 401
   B. 401; 708; 799; 798; 807
   C. 401; 708; 807; 798; 799
   D. 401; 708; 798; 799; 807

4. 12 x 2 =

   A. 16
   B. 28
   C. 18
   D. 24

5. What number do the Base Ten Blocks show?

   A. 108
   B. 180
   C. 18
   D. 8,100

6. 908 + 786 – 71 =

   A. 1,623
   B. 1,601
   C. 1,634
   D. 1,321

7. Use the clues to discover a 4-digit number. It has a 6 in the hundreds place. The other 3 digits are 4, 1, and 9. The greatest digit is in the ones place. The digit that is least is in the thousands place. What is the number?

   A. 1,699
   B. 1,649
   C. 1,409
   D. 1,609

8. Which picture shows $\frac{2}{3}$ shaded?

   A.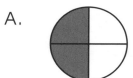

   B.

   C.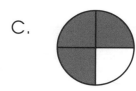

   D.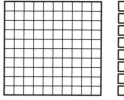

Assessment 14 (Lessons 131–140)   Name _____

1. $708 + 69 + 4,567 =$

A. 4,344
B. 5,206
C. 5,344
D. 3,546

2. $6 \times 9 =$

A. 15
B. 3
C. 54
D. 45

Use the bar graph to answer questions 3 and 4.

3. How many students in Grades 3, 4, and 5 participated in the fund-raiser?

A. 608
B. 905
C. 1,104
D. 799

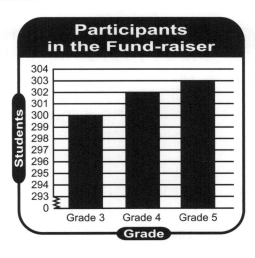

4. How many more students in Grades 4 and 5 combined participated in the fund-raiser than students in Grade 3 only?

A. 305
B. 906
C. 307
D. 454

5. The library has a selection of 2,334 books for students in the 3rd, 4th, and 5th grades. If 579 of the books are checked out, how many books does the library have available for students in the 3rd, 4th, and 5th grades?

A. 1,755
B. 2,913
C. 1,744
D. 3,011

6. Some friends volunteered to pick up litter in their neighborhood. Jordan worked 18 hours, Jami worked 36 hours, Quinton worked 24 hours, and Garrett worked 10 hours. How many hours did they work total?

A. 98
B. 78
C. 88
D. 70

7. $44 \div 11 =$

A. 5
B. 4
C. 11
D. 10

8. $14,345 + 17,899 =$

A. 3,554
B. 3,244
C. 32,244
D. 32,344

Assessment 15 (Lessons 141–150)   Name _____

1. What are the missing letters in the pattern?

    B, E, G, _____, L, O, _____

    A. H, P
    B. J, Q
    C. K, R
    D. J, P

2. 4,567 + 5,670 =

    A.   1,103
    B. 10,244
    C. 10,236
    D. 10,237

3. What are the missing numbers in the pattern?

    97, 92, _____, 82, _____, 72

    A. 85, 74
    B. 87, 72
    C. 87, 77
    D. 87, 92

4. Estimate to the nearest tens place.

    676 + 202 is about _____ .

    A. 870
    B. 800
    C. 900
    D. 880

5. Estimate to the nearest hundreds place.

    786 + 950 is about _____ .

    A. 1,800
    B. 1,740
    C. 2,000
    D. 1,700

6. Circle the best answer. Daniel is counting the number of game cards in his collection. He counts 5, 10, 15, 20, 25,…. By what number is Daniel counting?

    A.   5
    B. 10
    C. 15
    D.   2

7. Louisa has $705.67 in the bank. She earns $1.25 interest on her money. She later deposits an additional $54.50 into her account. How much money does Louisa have now?

    A. $661.43
    B. $761.42
    C. $771.02
    D. $706.92

8. 40 x 2 =

    A. 80
    B. 10
    C. 20
    D. 60

Assessment 16 (Lessons 151–160)   Name _____

1. A group of 4 boys are playing a game of tennis at 3 P.M. The boys have 84 balls. They plan to divide the balls equally among the players. How many tennis balls will each boy get?

A. 42
B. 14
C. 12
D. 21

2. 43,786 + 3,456 =

A. 47,242
B. 47,248
C. 51,206
D. 40,330

3. 19,234 – 6,544 =

A. 25,778
B. 12,690
C. 13,456
D. 27,989

4. 9 x 8 =

A. 72
B. 70
C. 99
D. 102

5. There are 81 shirts folded on the bed. The shirts are folded in 9 equal piles. How many shirts are in each pile?

A. 4
B. 12
C. 8
D. 9

6. What is the number in standard form?

three thousand six hundred nine

A. 3,609
B. 36,900
C. 39,600
D. 3,906

7. Which even number is greatest?

A. 9,003
B. 8,786
C. 12,347
D. 8,678

8. Janie has $33.47. She earns $7.75 for doing her chores. She then spends $12.50 going to the movies with a friend. How much money does Janie have now?

A. $41.22
B. $28.72
C. $29.72
D. $35.44

Assessment 17 (Lessons 161–170)

Name _____

1. $12 \times \underline{\hspace{1cm}} = 24$

   A. 2
   B. 10
   C. 12
   D. 4

2. Mary Beth earns $38.50 mowing lawns, $16.00 raking leaves, and $21.00 weeding gardens during the fall. She decides to put all of the money she earns in her savings account. How much money did Mary Beth earn in all?

   A. $75.50
   B. $59.50
   C. $70.75
   D. $49.90

3. $54 \div 6 =$

   A. 8
   B. 9
   C. 7
   D. 4

4. Circle the fraction that is equal to $\frac{4}{6}$.

   A. $\frac{1}{8}$

   B. $\frac{2}{3}$

   C. $\frac{3}{4}$

   D. $\frac{5}{6}$

5. $90 \div 9 =$

   A. 99
   B. 8
   C. 10
   D. 12

6. What is the number in standard form?

   $200,000 + 40,000 + 7,000 + 8$

   A. 251,008
   B. 247,808
   C. 247,800
   D. 247,008

7. Circle the answer choice that shows the number four hundred sixty-six thousand, five hundred one.

   A. 460,501
   B. 406,501
   C. 46,651
   D. 466,501

8. Use the clues to write a 4-digit number. The sum of the digits is 15. One of the digits is even. Three of the digits are odd. It has a 5 in the thousands place. The digit in the hundreds place is between 3 and 5. The digit in the ones place is greater than 4, but less than 6.

   A. 5,425
   B. 4,155
   C. 5,415
   D. 5,145

Assessment 18 (Lessons 171–180)

Name _____

1. Solve each number sentence. Then, use <, >, or = to make the number sentence true.

   44 + 71 – 19 _____ 64 + 33 – 11

   A. <
   B. >
   C. =

2. Which symbol will make the number sentence true?

   81,004 _____ 80,400

   A. <
   B. >
   C. =

3. Which symbol will make the number sentence true?

   14,564 _____ 15,434

   A. <
   B. >
   C. =

4. What is the missing number in the pattern?

   222, 249, _____, 303, 330

   A. 313
   B. 244
   C. 259
   D. 276

5. 14,567 + 21,456 =

   A. 34,567
   B. 36,023
   C. 36,003
   D. 37,541

6. 75 ÷ 5 =

   A. 7
   B. 10
   C. 15
   D. 12

7. 152 + 69 + 12 =

   A. 203
   B. 233
   C. 323
   D. 234

8. Delaney planted 8 rows of sunflowers in her garden. If there were 16 sunflowers in each row, how many sunflowers did Delaney plant in all?

   A. 182
   B. 168
   C. 120
   D. 128

Assessment Answer Keys

Assessment 1
1. B
2. B
3. D
4. C
5. A
6. A
7. B
8. C

Assessment 2
1. C
2. B
3. C
4. D
5. A
6. A
7. B
8. C

Assessment 3
1. B
2. D
3. D
4. C
5. C
6. A
7. C
8. D

Assessment 4
1. C
2. C
3. D
4. A
5. C
6. B
7. B
8. A

Assessment 5
1. A
2. B
3. C
4. D
5. A
6. A
7. C
8. C

Assessment 6
1. A
2. D
3. C
4. B
5. C
6. A
7. D
8. D

Assessment 7
1. B
2. B
3. C
4. D
5. B
6. B
7. C
8. D

Assessment 8
1. C
2. C
3. D
4. B
5. C
6. B
7. A
8. A

Assessment 9
1. D
2. D
3. A
4. B
5. C
6. B
7. A
8. A

Assessment 10
1. B
2. B
3. B
4. D
5. D
6. C
7. A
8. A

Assessment 11
1. D
2. A
3. B
4. C
5. C
6. C
7. A
8. C

Assessment 12
1. A
2. C
3. D
4. A
5. A
6. D
7. B
8. D

Assessment 13
1. A
2. C
3. D
4. D
5. A
6. A
7. B
8. D

Assessment 14
1. C
2. C
3. B
4. A
5. A
6. C
7. B
8. C

Assessment 15
1. B
2. D
3. C
4. D
5. A
6. A
7. B
8. A

Assessment 16
1. D
2. A
3. B
4. A
5. D
6. A
7. B
8. B

Assessment 17
1. A
2. A
3. B
4. B
5. C
6. D
7. D
8. C

Assessment 18
1. B
2. B
3. A
4. D
5. B
6. C
7. B
8. D

Real World Application 1

Look around your classroom and find a real-life pattern. On the lines below, write 2 sentences describing the pattern. Then, draw a picture of the pattern in the box below.

_____

_____

_____

_____

Real World Application 2

Label each column of the tally chart below with a day of the week. Ask your classmates to pick their favorite days of the week and make tally marks under the correct columns. Then, use the information to make a bar graph. Fill in the information from your tally chart on the bar graph. Title the chart and graph.

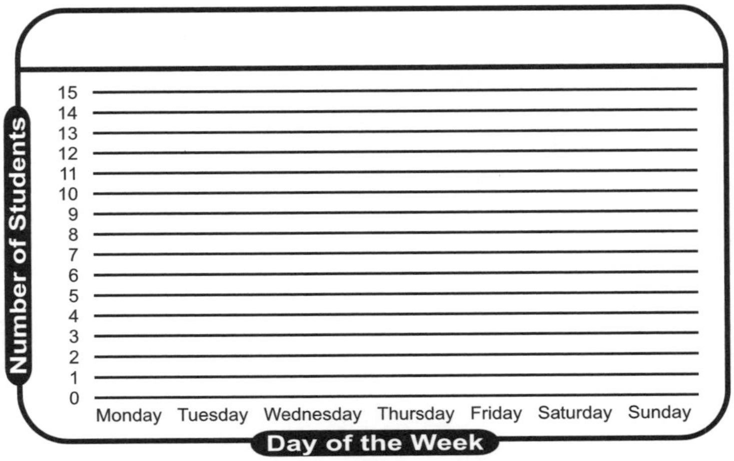

Number of Students: 15, 14, 13, 12, 11, 10, 9, 8, 7, 6, 5, 4, 3, 2, 1, 0

Monday Tuesday Wednesday Thursday Friday Saturday Sunday

Day of the Week

Real World Application 3

1. Poll some of your classmates. Ask them which of these 3 beverages they prefer: water, soda, or juice. Record your data on the tally chart below. Label and title your chart.

2. Record your data in the bar graph below. Title your graph.

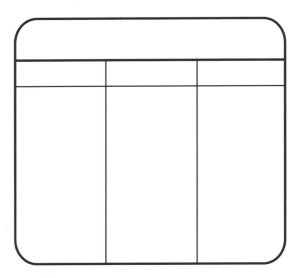

Number of Students

15
14
13
12
11
10
9
8
7
6
5
4
3
2
1
0

Water   Soda   Juice

Beverage

Real World Application 4

Fold a piece of paper into 4 equal sections. In each section, illustrate 1 of each of the following number sentences. Then, write a real-life word problem to go with each number sentence. Exchange papers with a classmate and see if you can solve each other's word problems.

1. $5 \times 2 =$

2. $13 - 4 =$

3. $21 + 7 =$

4. $2 \div 2 =$

Real World Application 5

Go on a geometry walk around your school. Find at least 1 of each shape. Write down the real-life object you found next to each shape name. Compare your findings with your classmates.

Cylinder _____

Cube _____

Cone _____

Pyramid _____

Sphere _____

Rectangular prism _____

Octagon _____

Circle _____

Rectangle _____

Square _____

Triangle _____

Real World Application 6

1. In a newspaper or magazine, find and circle 3 numbers that you find. On the lines below, write each of the numbers in word form, in standard form, and in expanded form.

2. Then, write a few sentences about the important role that numbers play in your daily life, and why it is important to be able to recognize the same number written in different forms.

_____

_____

_____

_____

_____

_____

Name _____

Real World Application 7

Make up an original multiplication word problem and write it on the lines provided. Write the answer to the problem in the box below.

_____

_____

_____

_____

_____

_____

Real World Application 8

Write a real-life, time-related word problem on the lines below. Remember to fill in a starting time on Clock A. Leave Clock B blank so that a classmate can try to solve your word problem.

_____

_____

Clock A

Clock B

Real World Application 9

Select 5 objects in your classroom to measure. Then, determine the weight and length of each object. Make sure to use the most appropriate units of measure. Share your findings with your class.

Object	Weight	Length
1.		
2.		
3.		
4.		
5.		

Real World Application 10

Did you know that you can check your subtraction work using addition? Look at the example below, then write and solve the addition problem you would use to solve each of the subtraction problems below.

Example: 72 – 68 = 4 and 68 + 4 = 72

1. 201 – 79 = _____ and _____ + _____ = _____

2. 1,657 – 908 = _____ and _____ + _____ = _____

3. 1,001 – 765 = _____ and _____ + _____ = _____

4. Try one on your own:
   _____ – _____ = _____ and _____ + _____ = _____

Real World Application 11

Make up an original division word problem and write it on the lines provided. Write the answer to the problem in the box below.

_____

_____

_____

_____

_____

_____

Real World Application 12

Think of a number between 1,000 and 5,000. Write the number on the back of a piece of paper. On the lines below, write at least three clues about your number. Then, see if a classmate can guess the number you have described.

_____

_____

_____

_____

_____

_____

_____